THE LIMITS TO GROWTH

POTOMAC ASSOCIATES is a nonpartisan research and analysis organization which seeks to encourage lively inquiry into critical issues of public policy. Its purpose is to heighten public understanding and improve public discourse on significant contemporary problems, national and international.

POTOMAC ASSOCIATES provides a forum for distinctive points of view through publication of timely studies and occasional papers by outstanding authorities in the United States and abroad. Although publication implies belief by Potomac Associates in the basic importance and validity of each study, views expressed are those of the author.

POTOMAC ASSOCIATES is a tax-exempt organization located at 1707 L Street, N.W., Washington, D.C. 20036. The following other Potomac Associates titles may be ordered from that address, but not from Universe Books:

HOPES AND FEARS OF THE AMERICAN PEOPLE
A NEW ISOLATIONISM: THREAT OR PROMISE?
U.S. HEALTH CARE: WHAT'S WRONG AND WHAT'S RIGHT?
STATE OF THE NATION 1972
A REORDERED WORLD: EMERGING INTERNATIONAL ECONOMIC PROBLEMS
BEYOND CONTAINMENT: U.S. FOREIGN POLICY IN TRANSITION
A NATION OBSERVED: PERSPECTIVES ON AMERICA'S WORLD ROLE
STATE OF THE NATION 1974

A POTOMAC ASSOCIATES BOOK

THE LIMITS TO GROWTH

A REPORT FOR
THE CLUB OF ROME'S PROJECT ON
THE PREDICAMENT OF MANKIND

SECOND EDITION

Donella H. Meadows
Dennis L. Meadows
Jørgen Randers
William W. Behrens III

Universe Books
NEW YORK

Published in the United States of America in 1974 by
Universe Books, 381 Park Avenue South, New York, N.Y. 10016

First edition:
First printing, March 1972
Fourteenth printing, February 1974
Second edition:
Third printing, June 1976

Library of Congress Catalog Card Number: ~~73-187907~~
Cloth edition: ISBN 0-87663-222-3
Paperback edition: ISBN 0-87663-918-X

Design by Hubert Leckie

Printed in the United States of America

To Dr. Aurelio Peccei, whose profound concern for humanity has inspired us and many others to think about the world's long-term problems

The MIT Project Team

Dr. Dennis L. Meadows, director, United States

DR. ALISON A. ANDERSON, United States *(pollution)*

DR. JAY M. ANDERSON, United States *(pollution)*

ILYAS BAYAR, Turkey *(agriculture)*

WILLIAM W. BEHRENS III, United States *(resources)*

FARHAD HAKIMZADEH, Iran *(population)*

DR. STEFFEN HARBORDT, Germany *(socio-political trends)*

JUDITH A. MACHEN, United States *(administration)*

DR. DONELLA H. MEADOWS, United States *(population)*

PETER MILLING, Germany *(capital)*

NIRMALA S. MURTHY, India *(population)*

ROGER F. NAILL, United States *(resources)*

JØRGEN RANDERS, Norway *(pollution)*

STEPHEN SHANTZIS, United States *(agriculture)*

JOHN A. SEEGER, United States *(administration)*

MARILYN WILLIAMS, United States *(documentation)*

DR. ERICH K. O. ZAHN, Germany *(agriculture)*

AUTHORS' NOTE ON THE SECOND EDITION

The two and a half tumultuous years that have elapsed since the publication of this text have not provided any information that would cause us to revise the general conclusions presented in our book. They have, however, given us the time to complete and publish two additional, technical reports on our work.* *The Limits to Growth* contains all the information required to evaluate the reasonableness of our general results. However, those wishing to extend our analysis, reproduce our computer plots, or use our models in teaching will require the second and third books as well.

To incorporate into World3 information obtained after the world model simulation runs for the first edition of *The Limits to Growth* were produced, we altered a few numerical parameters of World3 and modeled some dynamic phenomena in greater detail. Thus the model equations listed in *Dynamics*

* Dennis L. Meadows and Donella H. Meadows (eds.), *Toward Global Equilibrium* (Cambridge, Mass.: Wright-Allen Press, 1973).
Dennis L. Meadows *et al., Dynamics of Growth in a Finite World* (Cambridge, Mass.: Wright-Allen Press, 1974).

of Growth in a Finite World differ slightly from those employed to generate the illustrations in the first edition of *The Limits to Growth.* The changes affected neither the general behavior of the global model nor the conclusions derived from it. The changes did, however, alter the precise form of several simulation runs. To make both reports internally consistent, this edition of *The Limits to Growth* has been slightly revised to incorporate computer runs obtained from the version of our global model ultimately published in the technical report. The policy instructions required to reproduce the twelve computer runs in this book are included as an appendix to that report.

FOREWORD

IN APRIL 1968, a group of thirty individuals from ten countries—scientists, educators, economists, humanists, industrialists, and national and international civil servants—gathered in the Accademia dei Lincei in Rome. They met at the instigation of Dr. Aurelio Peccei, an Italian industrial manager, economist, and man of vision, to discuss a subject of staggering scope—the present and future predicament of man.

THE CLUB OF ROME

Out of this meeting grew The Club of Rome, an informal organization that has been aptly described as an "invisible college." Its purposes are to foster understanding of the varied but interdependent components—economic, political, natural, and social—that make up the global system in which we all live; to bring that new understanding to the attention of policy-makers and the public worldwide; and in this way to promote new policy initiatives and action.

The Club of Rome remains an informal international association, with a membership that has now grown to approximately seventy persons of twenty-five nationalities. None of its members holds public office, nor does the group seek to express any single ideological, political, or national point of view. All are united, however, by their overriding conviction that the major problems facing mankind are of such complexity and are so interrelated that traditional institutions and policies are no longer able to cope with them, nor even to come to grips with their full content.

The members of The Club of Rome have backgrounds as varied as their nationalities. Dr. Peccei, still the prime moving force within the group, is affiliated with Fiat and Olivetti and manages a consulting firm for economic and engineering development, Italconsult, one of the largest of its kind in Europe. Other leaders of The Club of Rome include: Hugo Thiemann, head of the Battelle Institute in Geneva; Alexander King, scientific director of the Organization for Economic Cooperation and Development; Saburo Okita, head of the Japan Economic Research Center in Tokyo; Eduard Pestel of the Technical University of Hannover, Germany; and Carroll Wilson of the Massachusetts Institute of Technology. Although membership in The Club of Rome is limited, and will not exceed one hundred, it is being expanded to include representatives of an ever greater variety of cultures, nationalities, and value systems.

THE PROJECT ON THE PREDICAMENT OF MANKIND

A series of early meetings of The Club of Rome culminated in the decision to initiate a remarkably ambitious undertaking —the Project on the Predicament of Mankind.

The intent of the project is to examine the complex of problems troubling men of all nations: poverty in the midst of plenty; degradation of the environment; loss of faith in institutions; uncontrolled urban spread; insecurity of employment; alienation of youth; rejection of traditional values; and inflation and other monetary and economic disruptions. These seemingly divergent parts of the "world problematique," as The Club of Rome calls it, have three characteristics in common: they occur to some degree in all societies; they contain technical, social, economic, and political elements; and, most important of all, they interact.

It is the predicament of mankind that man can perceive the problematique, yet, despite his considerable knowledge and skills, he does not understand the origins, significance, and interrelationships of its many components and thus is unable to devise effective responses. This failure occurs in large part because we continue to examine single items in the problematique without understanding that the whole is more than the sum of its parts, that change in one element means change in the others.

Phase One of the Project on the Predicament of Mankind took definite shape at meetings held in the summer of 1970 in Bern, Switzerland, and Cambridge, Massachusetts. At a two-week conference in Cambridge, Professor Jay Forrester of the Massachusetts Institute of Technology (MIT) presented a global model that permitted clear identification of many specific components of the problematique and suggested a technique for analyzing the behavior and relationships of the most important of those components. This presentation led to initiation of Phase One at MIT, where the pioneering work of Professor Forrester and others in the field of System Dynamics had created a body of expertise uniquely suited to the research demands.

The Phase One study was conducted by an international team, under the direction of Professor Dennis Meadows, with financial support from the Volkswagen Foundation. The team examined the five basic factors that determine, and therefore, ultimately limit, growth on this planet—population, agricultural production, natural resources, industrial production, and pollution. The research has now been completed. This book is the first account of the findings published for general readership.

A GLOBAL CHALLENGE

It is with genuine pride and pleasure that Potomac Associates joins with The Club of Rome and the MIT research team in the publication of *The Limits to Growth.*

We, like The Club of Rome, are a young organization, and we believe the Club's goals are very close to our own. Our purpose is to bring new ideas, new analyses, and new approaches to persistent problems—both national and international—to the attention of all those who care about and help determine the quality and direction of our life. We are delighted therefore to be able to make this bold and impressive work available through our book program.

We hope that *The Limits to Growth* will command critical attention and spark debate in all societies. We hope that it will encourage each reader to think through the consequences of continuing to equate growth with progress. And we hope that it will lead thoughtful men and women in all fields of endeavor to consider the need for concerted action now if we are to preserve the habitability of this planet for ourselves and our children.

William Watts, *President*
POTOMAC ASSOCIATES

CONTENTS

FIGURES

TABLES

INTRODUCTION

I do not wish to seem overdramatic, but I can only conclude from the information that is available to me as Secretary-General, that the Members of the United Nations have perhaps ten years left in which to subordinate their ancient quarrels and launch a global partnership to curb the arms race, to improve the human environment, to defuse the population explosion, and to supply the required momentum to development efforts. If such a global partnership is not forged within the next decade, then I very much fear that the problems I have mentioned will have reached such staggering proportions that they will be beyond our capacity to control.

U THANT, 1969

The problems U Thant mentions—the arms race, environmental deterioration, the population explosion, and economic stagnation—are often cited as the central, long-term problems of modern man. Many people believe that the future course of human society, perhaps even the survival of human society, depends on the speed and effectiveness with which the world responds to these issues. And yet only a small fraction of the world's population is actively concerned with understanding these problems or seeking their solutions.

HUMAN PERSPECTIVES

Every person in the world faces a series of pressures and problems that require his attention and action. These problems affect him at many different levels. He may spend much of his time trying to find tomorrow's food for himself and his family. He may be concerned about personal power or the power of the nation in which he lives. He may worry about a world war during his lifetime, or a war next week with a rival clan in his neighborhood.

These very different levels of human concern can be represented on a graph like that in figure 1. The graph has two dimensions, space and time. Every human concern can be located at some point on the graph, depending on how much geographical space it includes and how far it extends in time. Most people's worries are concentrated in the lower left-hand corner of the graph. Life for these people is difficult, and they must devote nearly all of their efforts to providing for themselves and their families, day by day. Other people think about and act on problems farther out on the space or time axes. The pressures they perceive involve not only themselves, but the community with which they identify. The actions they take extend not only days, but weeks or years into the future.

A person's time and space perspectives depend on his culture, his past experience, and the immediacy of the problems confronting him on each level. Most people must have successfully solved the problems in a smaller area before they move their concerns to a larger one. In general the larger the space and the longer the time associated with a problem, the smaller the number of people who are actually concerned with its solution.

There can be disappointments and dangers in limiting one's view to an area that is too small. There are many examples of a person striving with all his might to solve some immediate, local problem, only to find his efforts defeated by events occurring in a larger context. A farmer's carefully maintained

Figure 1 HUMAN PERSPECTIVES

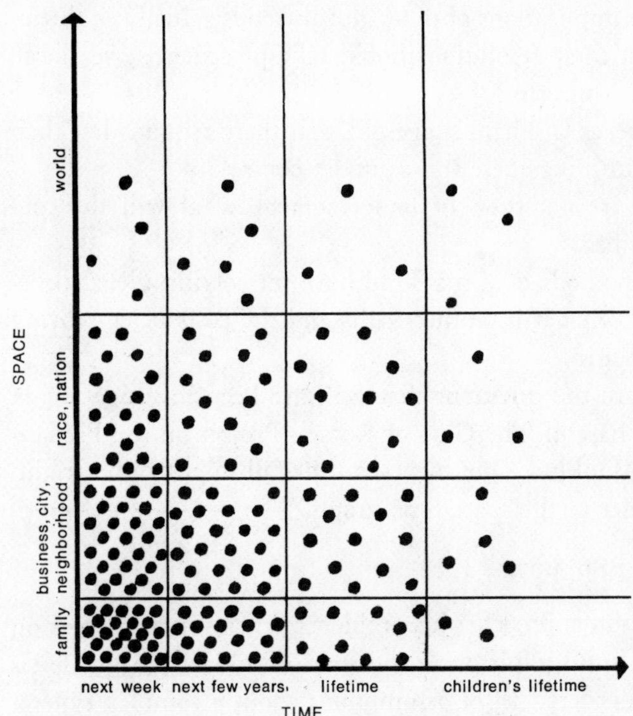

Although the perspectives of the world's people vary in space and in time, every human concern falls somewhere on the space-time graph. The majority of the world's people are concerned with matters that affect only family or friends over a short period of time. Others look farther ahead in time or over a larger area—a city or a nation. Only a very few people have a global perspective that extends far into the future.

fields can be destroyed by an international war. Local officials' plans can be overturned by a national policy. A country's economic development can be thwarted by a lack of world demand for its products. Indeed there is increasing concern today that most personal and national objectives may ultimately be frustrated by long-term, global trends such as those mentioned by U Thant.

Are the implications of these global trends actually so threatening that their resolution should take precedence over local, short-term concerns?

Is it true, as U Thant suggested, that there remains less than a decade to bring these trends under control?

If they are not brought under control, what will the consequences be?

What methods does mankind have for solving global problems, and what will be the results and the costs of employing each of them?

These are the questions that we have been investigating in the first phase of The Club of Rome's Project on the Predicament of Mankind. Our concerns thus fall in the upper right-hand corner of the space-time graph.

PROBLEMS AND MODELS

Every person approaches his problems, wherever they occur on the space-time graph, with the help of models. A model is simply an ordered set of assumptions about a complex system. It is an attempt to understand some aspect of the infinitely varied world by selecting from perceptions and past experience a set of general observations applicable to the problem at hand. A farmer uses a mental model of his land, his assets, market prospects, and past weather conditions to decide which crops to plant each year. A surveyor constructs a physical model—a map—to help in planning a road. An economist uses mathematical models to understand and predict the flow of international trade.

Decision-makers at every level unconsciously use mental models to choose among policies that will shape our future world. These mental models are, of necessity, very simple when compared with the reality from which they are abstracted. The human brain, remarkable as it is, can only keep track of a limited number of the complicated, simultaneous interactions that determine the nature of the real world.

We, too, have used a model. Ours is a formal, written model of the world.* It constitutes a preliminary attempt to improve our mental models of long-term, global problems by combining the large amount of information that is already in human minds and in written records with the new information-processing tools that mankind's increasing knowledge has produced—the scientific method, systems analysis, and the modern computer.

Our world model was built specifically to investigate five major trends of global concern—accelerating industrialization, rapid population growth, widespread malnutrition, depletion of nonrenewable resources, and a deteriorating environment. These trends are all interconnected in many ways, and their development is measured in decades or centuries, rather than in months or years. With the model we are seeking to understand the causes of these trends, their interrelationships, and their implications as much as one hundred years in the future.

The model we have constructed is, like every other model, imperfect, oversimplified, and unfinished. We are well aware of its shortcomings, but we believe that it is the most useful model now available for dealing with problems far out on the space-time graph. To our knowledge it is the only formal model in existence that is truly global in scope, that has a

* The prototype model on which we have based our work was designed by Professor Jay W. Forrester of the Massachusetts Institute of Technology. A description of that model has been published in his book *World Dynamics* (Cambridge, Mass.: Wright-Allen Press, 1971).

time horizon longer than thirty years, and that includes important variables such as population, food production, and pollution, not as independent entities, but as dynamically interacting elements, as they are in the real world.

Since ours is a formal, or mathematical, model it also has two important advantages over mental models. First, every assumption we make is written in a precise form so that it is open to inspection and criticism by all. Second, after the assumptions have been scrutinized, discussed, and revised to agree with our best current knowledge, their implications for the future behavior of the world system can be traced without error by a computer, no matter how complicated they become.

We feel that the advantages listed above make this model unique among all mathematical and mental world models available to us today. But there is no reason to be satisfied with it in its present form. We intend to alter, expand, and improve it as our own knowledge and the world data base gradually improve.

In spite of the preliminary state of our work, we believe it is important to publish the model and our findings now. Decisions are being made every day, in every part of the world, that will affect the physical, economic, and social conditions of the world system for decades to come. These decisions cannot wait for perfect models and total understanding. They will be made on the basis of some model, mental or written, in any case. We feel that the model described here is already sufficiently developed to be of some use to decision-makers. Furthermore, the basic behavior modes we have already observed in this model appear to be so fundamental and general that we do not expect our broad conclusions to be substantially altered by further revisions.

It is not the purpose of this book to give a complete, scientific description of all the data and mathematical equations included in the world model. Such a description can be found in the final technical report of our project.* Rather, in *The Limits to Growth* we summarize the main features of the model and our findings in a brief, nontechnical way. The emphasis is meant to be not on the equations or the intricacies of the model, but on what it tells us about the world. We have used a computer as a tool to aid our own understanding of the causes and consequences of the accelerating trends that characterize the modern world, but familiarity with computers is by no means necessary to comprehend or to discuss our conclusions. The implications of those accelerating trends raise issues that go far beyond the proper domain of a purely scientific document. They must be debated by a wider community than that of scientists alone. Our purpose here is to open that debate.

The following conclusions have emerged from our work so far. We are by no means the first group to have stated them. For the past several decades, people who have looked at the world with a global, long-term perspective have reached similar conclusions. Nevertheless, the vast majority of policy-makers seems to be actively pursuing goals that are inconsistent with these results.

* The detailed data and assumptions underlying our model and the computer equations used to generate the model runs employed in this text are provided in Dennis L. Meadows *et al., Dynamics of Growth in a Finite World* (Cambridge, Mass.: Wright-Allen Press, 1974).

Our conclusions are:

1. If the present growth trends in world population, industrialization, pollution, food production, and resource depletion continue unchanged, the limits to growth on this planet will be reached sometime within the next one hundred years. The most probable result will be a rather sudden and uncontrollable decline in both population and industrial capacity.

2. It is possible to alter these growth trends and to establish a condition of ecological and economic stability that is sustainable far into the future. The state of global equilibrium could be designed so that the basic material needs of each person on earth are satisfied and each person has an equal opportunity to realize his individual human potential.

3. If the world's people decide to strive for this second outcome rather than the first, the sooner they begin working to attain it, the greater will be their chances of success.

These conclusions are so far-reaching and raise so many questions for further study that we are quite frankly overwhelmed by the enormity of the job that must be done. We hope that this book will serve to interest other people, in many fields of study and in many countries of the world, to raise the space and time horizons of their concerns and to join us in understanding and preparing for a period of great transition—the transition from growth to global equilibrium.

CHAPTER I

THE NATURE OF EXPONENTIAL GROWTH

People at present think that five sons are not too many and each son has five sons also, and before the death of the grandfather there are already 25 descendants. Therefore people are more and wealth is less; they work hard and receive little.

HAN FEI-TZU, ca. 500 B.C.

All five elements basic to the study reported here—population, food production, industrialization, pollution, and consumption of nonrenewable natural resources—are increasing. The amount of their increase each year follows a pattern that mathematicians call exponential growth. Nearly all of mankind's current activities, from use of fertilizer to expansion of cities, can be represented by exponential growth curves (see figures 2 and 3). Since much of this book deals with the causes and implications of exponential growth curves, it is important to begin with an understanding of their general characteristics.

THE MATHEMATICS OF EXPONENTIAL GROWTH

Most people are accustomed to thinking of growth as a *linear* process. A quantity is growing linearly when it increases by a

Figure 2 WORLD FERTILIZER CONSUMPTION

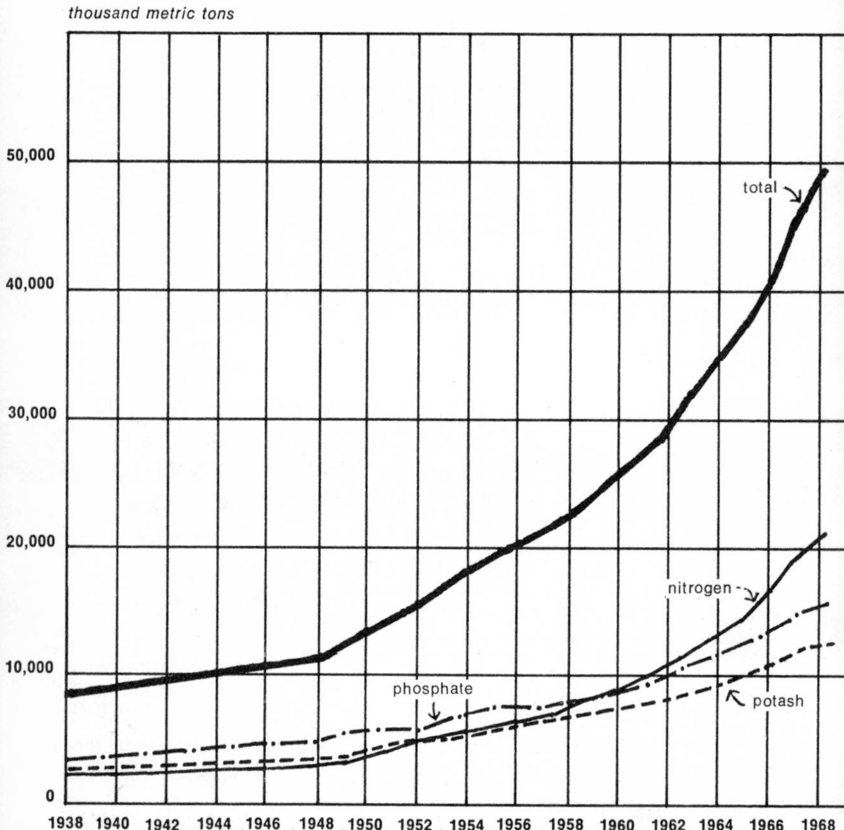

World fertilizer consumption is increasing exponentially, with a doubling time of about 10 years. Total use is now five times greater than it was during World War II.

NOTE: Figures do not include the USSR or the People's Republic of China.

SOURCES: UN Department of Economic and Social Affairs, *Statistical Yearbook 1955, Statistical Yearbook 1960,* and *Statistical Yearbook 1970* (New York: United Nations, 1956, 1961, and 1971).

constant amount in a constant time period. For example, a child who becomes one inch taller each year is growing linearly. If a miser hides $10 each year under his mattress, his

Figure 3 WORLD URBAN POPULATION

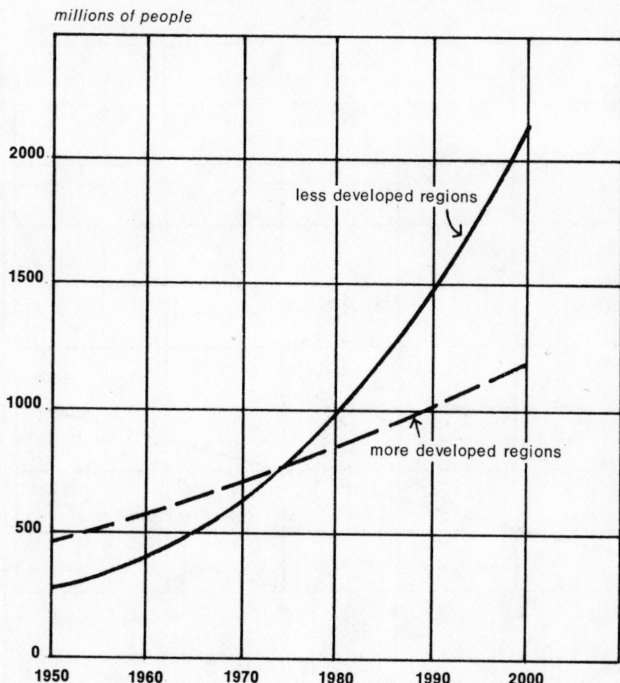

Total urban population is expected to increase exponentially in the less developed regions of the world, but almost linearly in the more developed regions. Present average doubling time for city populations in less developed regions is 15 years.

SOURCE: UN Department of Economic and Social Affairs, *The World Population Situation in 1970* (New York: United Nations, 1971).

horde of money is also increasing in a linear way. The amount of increase each year is obviously not affected by the size of the child nor the amount of money already under the mattress.

A quantity exhibits *exponential* growth when it increases by a constant percentage of the whole in a constant time period. A colony of yeast cells in which each cell divides into two cells every 10 minutes is growing exponentially. For each single cell, after 10 minutes there will be two cells, an increase

Figure 4 THE GROWTH OF SAVINGS

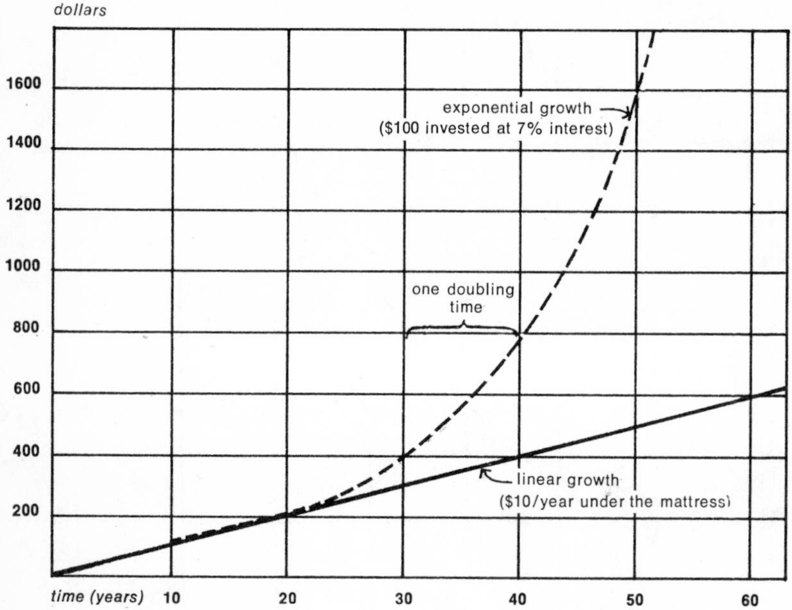

If a miser hides $10 each year under his mattress, his savings will grow linearly, as shown by the lower curve. If, after 10 years, he invests his $100 at 7 percent interest, that $100 will grow exponentially, with a doubling time of 10 years.

of 100 percent. After the next 10 minutes there will be four cells, then eight, then sixteen. If a miser takes $100 from his mattress and invests it at 7 percent (so that the total amount accumulated increases by 7 percent each year), the invested money will grow much faster than the linearly increasing stock under the mattress (see figure 4). The amount added each year to a bank account or each 10 minutes to a yeast colony is not constant. It continually increases, as the total accumulated amount increases. Such exponential growth is a common process in biological, financial, and many other systems of the world.

Common as it is, exponential growth can yield surprising results—results that have fascinated mankind for centuries. There is an old Persian legend about a clever courtier who presented a beautiful chessboard to his king and requested that the king give him in return 1 grain of rice for the first square on the board, 2 grains for the second square, 4 grains for the third, and so forth. The king readily agreed and ordered rice to be brought from his stores. The fourth square of the chessboard required 8 grains, the tenth square took 512 grains, the fifteenth required 16,384, and the twenty-first square gave the courtier more than a million grains of rice. By the fortieth square a million million rice grains had to be brought from the storerooms. The king's entire rice supply was exhausted long before he reached the sixty-fourth square. Exponential increase is deceptive because it generates immense numbers very quickly.

A French riddle for children illustrates another aspect of exponential growth—the apparent suddenness with which it approaches a fixed limit. Suppose you own a pond on which a water lily is growing. The lily plant doubles in size each day. If the lily were allowed to grow unchecked, it would completely cover the pond in 30 days, choking off the other forms of life in the water. For a long time the lily plant seems small, and so you decide not to worry about cutting it back until it covers half the pond. On what day will that be? On the twenty-ninth day, of course. You have one day to save your pond.*

It is useful to think of exponential growth in terms of *doubling time,* or the time it takes a growing quantity to

* We are indebted to M. Robert Lattes for telling us this riddle.

double in size. In the case of the lily plant described above, the doubling time is 1 day. A sum of money left in a bank at 7 percent interest will double in 10 years. There is a simple mathematical relationship between the interest rate, or rate of growth, and the time it will take a quantity to double in size. The doubling time is approximately equal to 70 divided by the growth rate, as illustrated in table 1.

Table 1 DOUBLING TIME

Growth rate (% per year)	*Doubling time (years)*
0.1	700
0.5	140
1.0	70
2.0	35
4.0	18
5.0	14
7.0	10
10.0	7

MODELS AND EXPONENTIAL GROWTH

Exponential growth is a dynamic phenomenon, which means that it involves elements that change over time. In simple systems, like the bank account or the lily pond, the cause of exponential growth and its future course are relatively easy to understand. When many different quantities are growing simultaneously in a system, however, and when all the quantities are interrelated in a complicated way, analysis of the causes of growth and of the future behavior of the system becomes very difficult indeed. Does population growth cause industrialization or does industrialization cause population growth? Is either one singly responsible for increasing pollution, or are they both responsible? Will more food production result in more population? If any one of these elements grows slower or faster, what will happen to the growth rates of all the others? These very questions are being debated in many parts of the world today. The answers can be found through a better understanding of the entire complex system that unites all of these important elements.

Over the course of the last 30 years there has evolved at the Massachusetts Institute of Technology a new method for understanding the dynamic behavior of complex systems. The method is called System Dynamics.* The basis of the method is the recognition that the *structure* of any system—the many circular, interlocking, sometimes time-delayed relationships among its components—is often just as important in determining its behavior as the individual components themselves. The world model described in this book is a System Dynamics model.

Dynamic modeling theory indicates that any exponentially growing quantity is somehow involved with a *positive feedback loop.* A positive feedback loop is sometimes called a "vicious circle." An example is the familiar wage-price spiral—wages increase, which causes prices to increase, which leads to demands for higher wages, and so forth. In a positive feedback loop a chain of cause-and-effect relationships closes on itself, so that increasing any one element in the loop will start a sequence of changes that will result in the originally changed element being increased even more.

---

* A detailed description of the method of System Dynamics analysis is presented in J. W. Forrester's *Industrial Dynamics* (Cambridge, Mass.: MIT Press, 1961) and *Principles of Systems* (Cambridge, Mass.: Wright-Allen Press, 1968).

The positive feedback loop that accounts for exponential increase of money in a bank account can be represented like this:

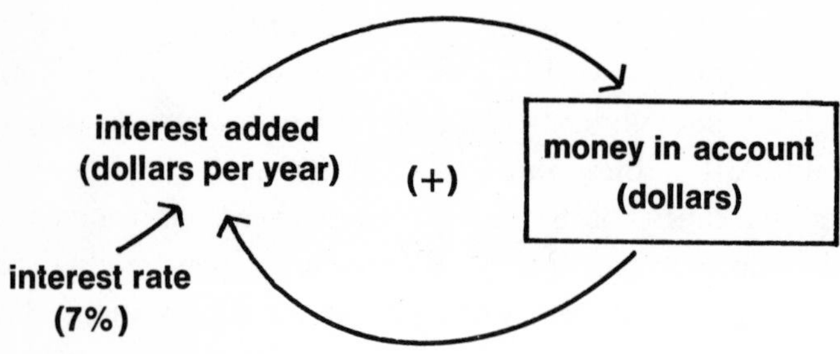

Suppose $100 is deposited in the account. The first year's interest is 7 percent of $100, or $7, which is added to the account, making the total $107. The next year's interest is 7 percent of $107, or $7.49, which makes a new total of $114.49. One year later the interest on that amount will be more than $8.00. The more money there is in the account, the more money will be added each year in interest. The more is added, the more there will be in the account the next year causing even more to be added in interest. And so on. As we go around and around the loop, the accumulated money in the account grows exponentially. The rate of interest (constant at 7 percent) determines the gain around the loop, or the rate at which the bank account grows.

We can begin our dynamic analysis of the long-term world situation by looking for the positive feedback loops underlying the exponential growth in the five physical quantities we have already mentioned. In particular, the growth rates of two of these elements—population and industrialization—are of interest, since the goal of many development policies is to encourage the growth of the latter relative to the former. The

Figure 5 WORLD POPULATION

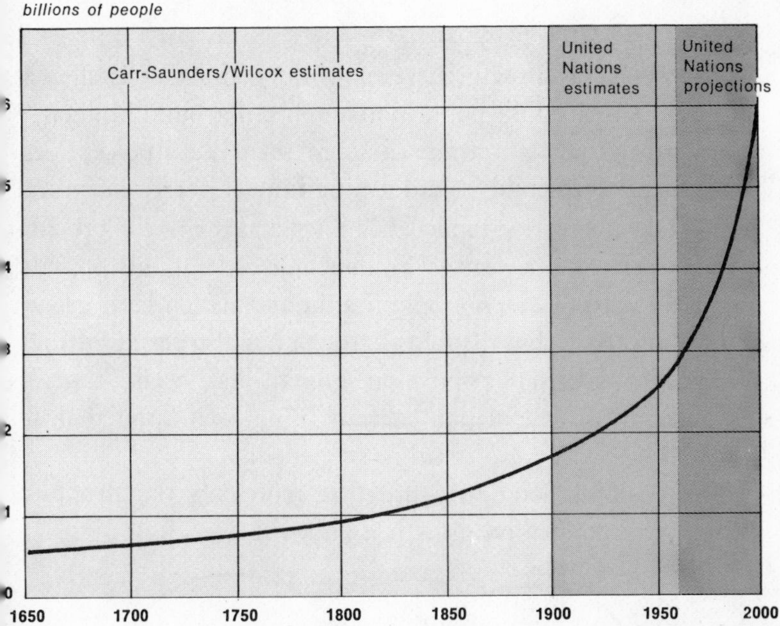

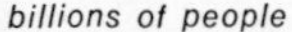

World population since 1650 has been growing exponentially at an increasing rate. Estimated population in 1970 is already slightly higher than the projection illustrated here (which was made in 1958). The present world population growth rate is about 2.1 percent per year, corresponding to a doubling time of 33 years.

SOURCE: Donald J. Bogue, *Principles of Demography* (New York: John Wiley and Sons, 1969).

two basic positive feedback loops that account for exponential population and industrial growth are simple in principle. We will describe their basic structures in the next few pages. The many interconnections between these two positive feedback loops act to amplify or to diminish the action of the loops, to couple or uncouple the growth rates of population and of industry. These interconnections constitute the rest of the world model and their description will occupy much of the rest of this book.

WORLD POPULATION GROWTH

The exponential growth curve of world population is shown in figure 5. In 1650 the population numbered about 0.5 billion,* and it was growing at a rate of approximately 0.3 percent per year.[1] That corresponds to a doubling time of nearly 250 years. In 1970 the population totaled 3.6 billion and the rate of growth was 2.1 percent per year.[2] The doubling time at this growth rate is 33 years. Thus, not only has the population been growing exponentially, but the rate of growth has also been growing. We might say that population growth has been "super"-exponential; the population curve is rising even faster than it would if growth were strictly exponential.

The feedback loop structure that represents the dynamic behavior of population growth is shown below.

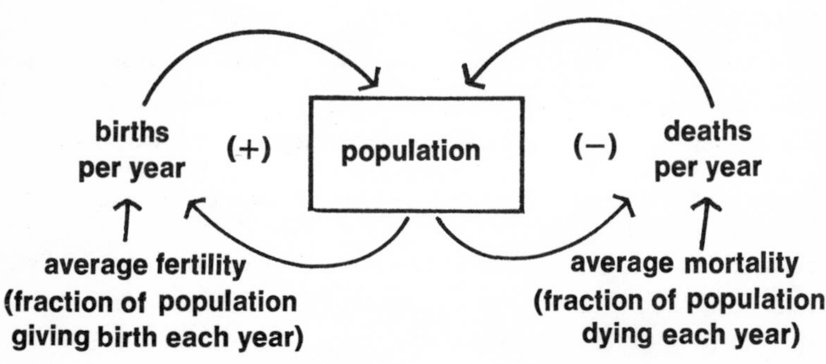

On the left is the positive feedback loop that accounts for the observed exponential growth. In a population with constant average fertility, the larger the population, the more babies will be born each year. The more babies, the larger the popula-

* The word "billion" in this book will be used to mean 1000 million, i.e. the European "milliard."

[1] Notes begin on page 201.

tion will be the following year. After a delay to allow those babies to grow up and become parents, even more babies will be born, swelling the population still further. Steady growth will continue as long as average fertility remains constant. If, in addition to sons, each woman has on the average two female children, for example, and each of them grows up to have two more female children, the population will double each generation. The growth rate will depend on both the average fertility and the length of the delay between generations. Fertility is not necessarily constant, of course, and in chapter III we will discuss some of the factors that cause it to vary.

There is another feedback loop governing population growth, shown on the right side of the diagram above. It is a *negative feedback loop.* Whereas positive feedback loops generate runaway growth, negative feedback loops tend to regulate growth and to hold a system in some stable state. They behave much as a thermostat does in controlling the temperature of a room. If the temperature falls, the thermostat activates the heating system, which causes the temperature to rise again. When the temperature reaches its limit, the thermostat cuts off the heating system, and the temperature begins to fall again. In a negative feedback loop a change in one element is propagated around the circle until it comes back to change that element in a direction *opposite* to the initial change.

The negative feedback loop controlling population is based upon average mortality, a reflection of the general health of the population. The number of deaths each year is equal to the total population times the average mortality (which we might think of as the average probability of death at any age).

An increase in the size of a population with constant average mortality will result in more deaths per year. More deaths will leave fewer people in the population, and so there will be fewer deaths the next year. If on the average 5 percent of the population dies each year, there will be 500 deaths in a population of 10,000 in one year. Assuming no births for the moment, that would leave 9,500 people the next year. If the probability of death is still 5 percent, there will be only 475 deaths in this smaller population, leaving 9,025 people. The next year there will be only 452 deaths. Again, there is a delay in this feedback loop because the mortality rate is a function of the average age of the population. Also, of course, mortality even at a given age is not necessarily constant.

If there were no deaths in a population, it would grow exponentially by the positive feedback loop of births, as shown below. If there were no births, the population would decline

to zero because of the negative feedback loop of deaths, also as shown below. Since every real population experiences both

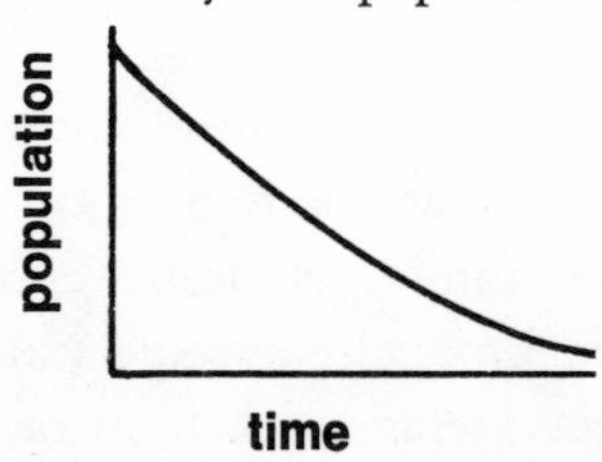

births and deaths, as well as varying fertility and mortality, the dynamic behavior of populations governed by these two interlocking feedback loops can become fairly complicated.

What has caused the recent super-exponential rise in world population? Before the industrial revolution both fertility and mortality were comparatively high and irregular. The birth rate generally exceeded the death rate only slightly, and population grew exponentially, but at a very slow and uneven rate. In 1650 the average lifetime of most populations in the world was only about 30 years. Since then, mankind has developed many practices that have had profound effects on the population growth system, especially on mortality rates. With the spread of modern medicine, public health techniques, and new methods of growing and distributing foods, death rates have fallen around the world. World average life expectancy is currently about 53 years [3] and still rising. On a world average the gain around the positive feedback loop (fertility) has decreased only slightly while the gain around the negative feedback loop (mortality) is decreasing. The result is an increasing dominance of the positive feedback loop and the sharp exponential rise in population pictured in figure 5.

What about the population of the future? How might we extend the population curve of figure 5 into the twenty-first century? We will have more to say about this in chapters III and IV. For the moment we can safely conclude that because of the delays in the controlling feedback loops, especially the positive loop of births, there is no possibility of leveling off the population growth curve before the year 2000, even with the most optimistic assumption of decreasing fertility. Most of the prospective parents of the year 2000 have already been born. Unless there is a sharp rise in mortality,

Figure 6 WORLD INDUSTRIAL PRODUCTION

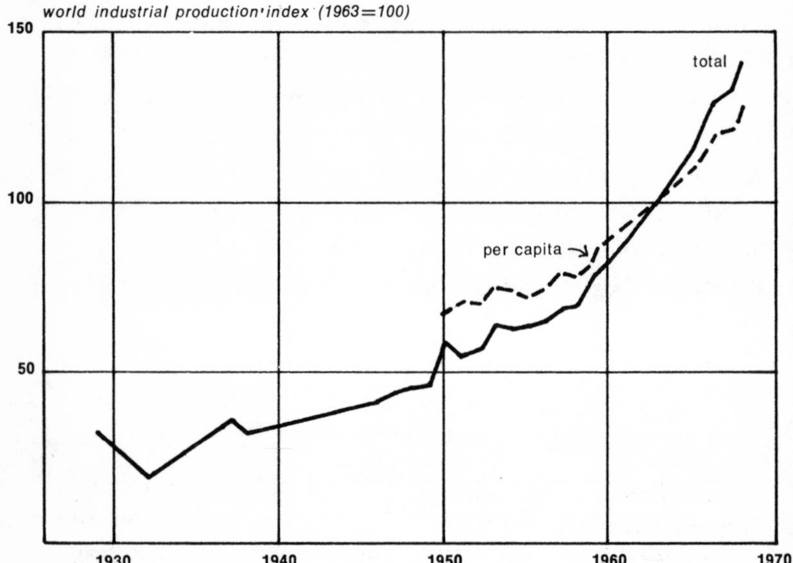

World industrial production, relative to the base year 1963, also shows a clear exponential increase despite small fluctuations. The 1963-68 average growth rate of total production is 7 percent per year. The per capita growth rate is 5 percent per year.

SOURCES: UN Department of Economic and Social Affairs, *Statistical Yearbook 1956* and *Statistical Yearbook 1969* (New York: United Nations, 1957 and 1970).

which mankind will certainly strive mightily to avoid, we can look forward to a world population of around 7 billion persons in 30 more years. And if we continue to succeed in lowering mortality with no better success in lowering fertility than we have accomplished in the past, in 60 years there will be four people in the world for every one person living today.

WORLD ECONOMIC GROWTH

A second quantity that has been increasing in the world even faster than human population is industrial output. Figure 6 shows the expansion of world industrial production since 1930, with 1963 production as the base of reference. The average growth rate from 1963 to 1968 was 7 percent per year, or 5 percent per year on a per capita basis.

What is the positive feedback loop that accounts for exponential growth of industrial output? The dynamic structure, diagramed below, is actually very similar to the one we have already described for the population system.

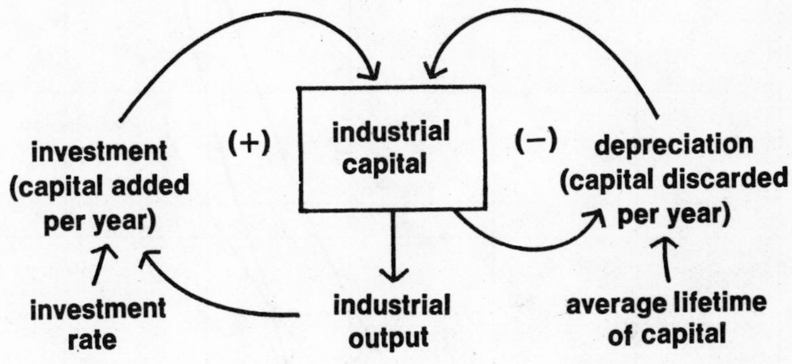

With a given amount of industrial capital (factories, trucks, tools, machines, etc.), a certain amount of manufactured output each year is possible. The output actually produced is also dependent on labor, raw materials, and other inputs. For the moment we will assume that these other inputs are sufficient, so that capital is the limiting factor in production. (The world model does include these other inputs.) Much of each year's output is consumable goods, such as textiles, automobiles, and houses, that leave the industrial system. But some fraction of the production is more capital—looms, steel mills, lathes—which is an investment to increase the capital stock. Here we have another positive feedback loop. More capital creates more

Figure 7 ECONOMIC GROWTH RATES

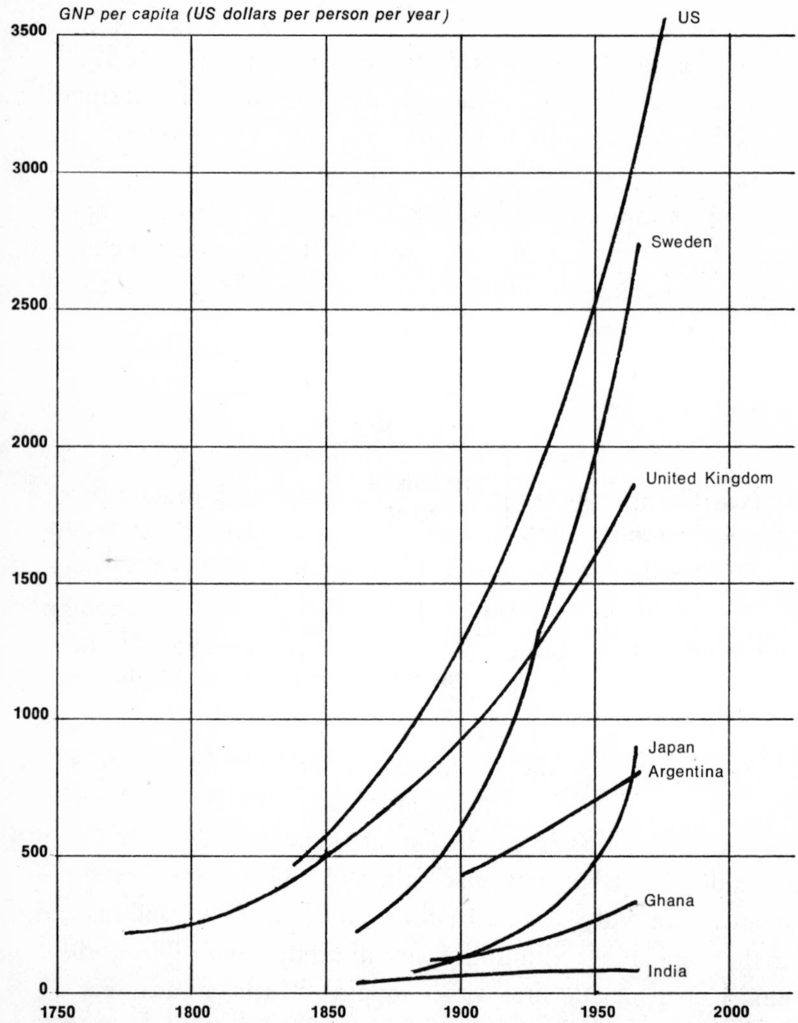

The economic growth of individual nations indicates that differences in exponential growth rates are widening the economic gap between rich and poor countries.

SOURCE: Simon Kuznets, *Economic Growth of Nations* (Cambridge, Mass.: Harvard University Press, 1971).

output, some variable fraction of the output is investment, and more investment means more capital. The new, larger capital stock generates even more output, and so on. There are also delays in this feedback loop, since the production of a major piece of industrial capital, such as an electrical generating plant or a refinery, can take several years.

Capital stock is not permanent. As capital wears out or becomes obsolete, it is discarded. To model this situation we must introduce into the capital system a negative feedback loop accounting for capital depreciation. The more capital there is, the more wears out on the average each year; and the more that wears out, the less there will be the next year. This negative feedback loop is exactly analogous to the death rate loop in the population system. As in the population system, the positive loop is strongly dominant in the world today, and the world's industrial capital stock is growing exponentially.

Since industrial output is growing at 7 percent per year and population only at 2 percent per year, it might appear that dominant positive feedback loops are a cause for rejoicing. Simple extrapolation of those growth rates would suggest that the material standard of living of the world's people will double within the next 14 years. Such a conclusion, however, often includes the implicit assumption that the world's growing industrial output is evenly distributed among the world's citizens. The fallacy of this assumption can be appreciated when the per capita economic growth rates of some individual nations are examined (see figure 7).

Most of the world's industrial growth plotted in figure 6 is actually taking place in the already industrialized countries, where the rate of population growth is comparatively low.

Table 2 ECONOMIC AND POPULATION GROWTH RATES

Country	*Population (1968) (million)*	*Average annual growth rate of population (1961–68) (% per year)*	*GNP per capita (1968) (US dollars)*	*Average annual growth rate of GNP per capita (1961–68) (% per year)*
People's Republic of China *	730	1.5	90	0.3
India	524	2.5	100	1.0
USSR *	238	1.3	1,100	5.8
United States	201	1.4	3,980	3.4
Pakistan	123	2.6	100	3.1
Indonesia	113	2.4	100	0.8
Japan	101	1.0	1,190	9.9
Brazil	88	3.0	250	1.6
Nigeria	63	2.4	70	—0.3
Federal Republic of Germany	60	1.0	1,970	3.4

* The International Bank for Reconstruction and Development qualifies its estimates for China and the USSR with the following statement: "Estimates of GNP per capita and its growth rate have a wide margin of error mainly because of the problems in deriving the GNP at factor cost from net material product and in converting the GNP estimate into US dollars." United Nations estimates are in general agreement with those of the IBRD.

SOURCE: *World Bank Atlas* (Washington,DC: International Bank for Reconstruction and Development, 1970).

The most revealing possible illustration of that fact is a simple table listing the economic and population growth rates of the ten most populous nations of the world, where 64 percent of the world's population currently lives. Table 2 makes very clear the basis for the saying, "The rich get richer and the poor get children."

It is unlikely that the rates of growth listed in table 2 will continue unchanged even until the end of this century. Many factors will change in the next 30 years. The end of civil disturbance in Nigeria, for example, will probably increase the economic growth rate there, while the onset of civil disturbance and then war in Pakistan has already interfered with economic growth there. Let us recognize, however, that the growth rates listed above are the products of a complicated social and economic system that is essentially stable and that is likely to change slowly rather than quickly, except in cases of severe social disruption.

It is a simple matter of arithmetic to calculate extrapolated values for gross national product (GNP) per capita from now until the year 2000 on the assumption that relative growth rates of population and GNP will remain roughly the same in these ten countries. The result of such a calculation appears in table 3. The values shown there will almost certainly *not* actually be realized. They are not predictions. The values merely indicate the general direction our system, as it is currently structured, is taking us. *They demonstrate that the process of*

Table 3 EXTRAPOLATED GNP FOR THE YEAR 2000

Country	*GNP per capita (in US dollars *)*
People's Republic of China	100
India	140
USSR	6,330
United States	11,000
Pakistan	250
Indonesia	130
Japan	23,200
Brazil	440
Nigeria	60
Federal Republic of Germany	5,850

* Based on the 1968 dollar with no allowance for inflation.

economic growth, as it is occurring today, is inexorably widening the absolute gap between the rich and the poor nations of the world.

Most people intuitively and correctly reject extrapolations like those shown in table 3, because the results appear ridiculous. It must be recognized, however, that in rejecting extrapolated values, one is also rejecting the assumption that there will be *no change* in the system. If the extrapolations in table 3 do not actually come to pass, it will be because the balance between the positive and negative feedback loops determining the growth rates of population and capital in each nation has been altered. Fertility, mortality, the capital investment rate, the capital depreciation rate—any or all may change. In postulating any different outcome from the one shown in table 3, one must specify which of these factors is likely to change, by how much, and when. These are exactly the questions we are addressing with our model, not on a national basis, but on an aggregated global one.

To speculate with any degree of realism on future growth rates of population and industrial capital, we must know something more about the other factors in the world that interact with the population-capital system. We shall begin by asking a very basic set of questions.

Can the growth rates of population and capital presented in table 3 be physically sustained in the world? How many people can be provided for on this earth, at what level of wealth, and for how long? To answer these questions, we must look in detail at those systems in the world which provide the physical support for population and economic growth.

CHAPTER II

THE LIMITS TO EXPONENTIAL GROWTH

For which of you, intending to build a tower, sitteth not down first, and counteth the cost, whether he have sufficient to finish it?

LUKE 14:28

What will be needed to sustain world economic and population growth until, and perhaps even beyond, the year 2000? The list of necessary ingredients is long, but it can be divided roughly into two main categories.

The first category includes the *physical* necessities that support all physiological and industrial activity—food, raw materials, fossil and nuclear fuels, and the ecological systems of the planet which absorb wastes and recycle important basic chemical substances. These ingredients are in principle tangible, countable items, such as arable land, fresh water, metals, forests, the oceans. In this chapter we will assess the world's stocks of these physical resources, since they are the ultimate determinants of the limits to growth on this earth.

The second category of necessary ingredients for growth consists of the *social* necessities. Even if the earth's physical systems are capable of supporting a much larger, more economically developed population, the actual growth of the economy and of the population will depend on such factors as peace and social stability, education and employment, and steady technological progress. These factors are much more difficult to assess or to predict. Neither this book nor our world model at this stage in its development can deal explicitly with these social factors, except insofar as our information about the quantity and distribution of physical supplies can indicate possible future social problems.

Food, resources, and a healthy environment are necessary but not sufficient conditions for growth. Even if they are abundant, growth may be stopped by social problems. Let us assume for the moment, however, that the best possible social conditions will prevail. How much growth will the physical system then support? The answer we obtain will give us some estimate of the upper limits to population and capital growth, but no guarantee that growth will actually proceed that far.

FOOD

In Zambia, in Africa, 260 of every thousand babies born are dead before their first birthday. In India and Pakistan the ratio is 140 of every thousand; in Colombia it is 82. Many more die before they reach school age; others during the early school years.

Where death certificates are issued for preschool infants in the poor countries, death is generally attributed to measles, pneumonia, dysentery, or some other disease. In fact these children are more likely to be the victims of malnutrition.[4]

No one knows exactly how many of the world's people are inadequately nourished today, but there is general agreement that the number is large—perhaps 50 to 60 percent of the population of the less industrialized countries,[5] which means one-third of the population of the world. Estimates by the

Figure 8 PROTEIN AND CALORIC INTAKE

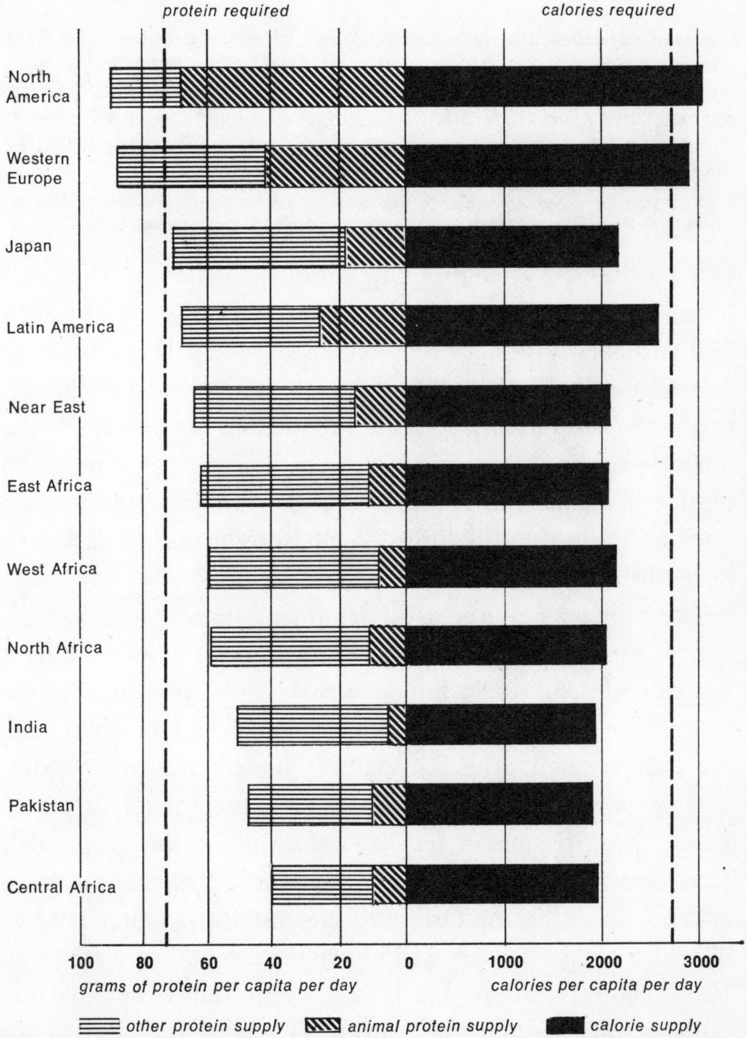

Daily protein and calorie requirements are not being supplied to most areas of the world. Inequalities of distribution exist not only among regions, as shown here, but also within regions. According to the UN Food and Agriculture Organization, areas of greatest shortage include the

"Andean countries, the semi-arid stretches of Africa and the Near East, and some densely populated countries of Asia." Lines indicating calories and proteins required are those estimated for North Americans. The assumption has been made that if diets in other regions were sufficient to allow people to reach full potential body weight, requirements would be the same everywhere.

SOURCE: UN Food and Agriculture Organization, *Provisional Indicative World Plan for Agricultural Development* (Rome: UN Food and Agriculture Organization, 1970).

UN Food and Agriculture Organization (FAO) indicate that in most of the developing countries basic caloric requirements, and particularly protein requirements, are not being supplied (see figure 8). Furthermore, although total world agricultural production is increasing, food production *per capita* in the nonindustrialized countries is barely holding constant at its present inadequate level (see figure 9). Do these rather dismal statistics mean that the limits of food production on the earth have already been reached?

The primary resource necessary for producing food is land. Recent studies indicate that there are, at most, about 3.2 billion hectares of land (7.86 billion acres) potentially suitable for agriculture on the earth.[6] Approximately half of that land, the richest, most accessible half, is under cultivation today. The remaining land will require immense capital inputs to reach, clear, irrigate, or fertilize before it is ready to produce food. Recent costs of developing new land have ranged from $215 to $5,275 per hectare. Average cost for opening land in unsettled areas has been $1,150 per hectare.[7] According to an FAO report, opening more land to cultivation is not economically feasible, even given the pressing need for food in the world today:

In Southern Asia . . . in some countries in Eastern Asia, in the Near East and North Africa, and in certain parts of Latin America and Africa . . . there is almost no scope for expanding the arable area.

Figure 9 FOOD PRODUCTION

regional average food production index (1952 - 56 = 100)

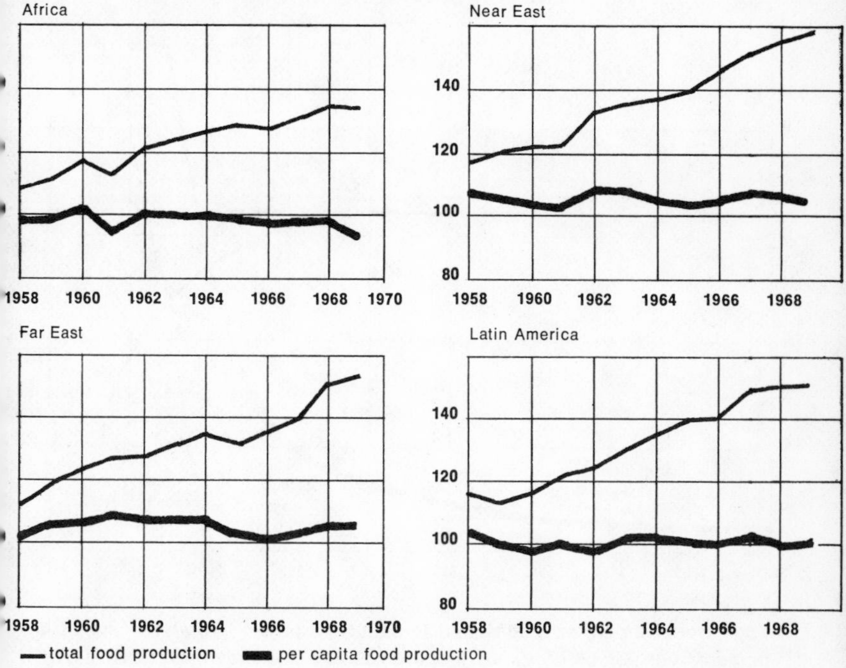

Africa

1958 1960 1962 1964 1966 1968 1970

Near East

140
120
100
80

1958 1960 1962 1964 1966 1968

Far East

1958 1960 1962 1964 1966 1968 1970

Latin America

140
120
100
80

1958 1960 1962 1964 1966 1968

total food production — per capita food production

Total food production in the nonindustrialized regions of the world has risen at about the same rate as the population. Thus food production ***per capita*** *has remained nearly constant, at a low level.*

SOURCE: UN Food and Agriculture Organization, *The State of Food and Agriculture 1970* (Rome: UN Food and Agriculture Organization, 1970).

. . . In the dryer regions it will even be necessary to return to permanent pasture the land which is marginal or submarginal for cultivation. In most of Latin America and Africa South of the Sahara there are still considerable possibilities for expanding cultivated area, but the costs of development are high and it will be often more economical to intensify utilization of the areas already settled.[8]

If the world's people did decide to pay the high capital costs, to cultivate all possible arable land, and to produce as much food as possible, how many people could theoretically be fed?

Figure 10 ARABLE LAND

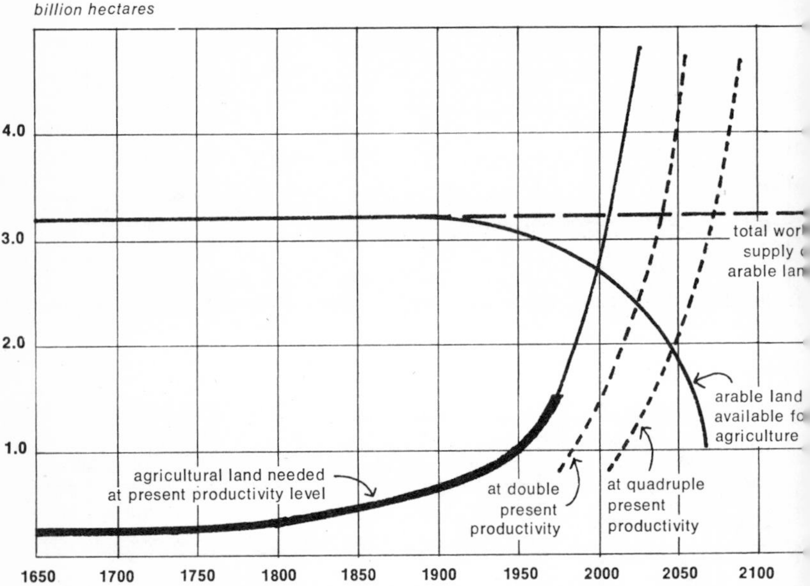

Total world supply of arable land is about 3.2 billion hectares. About 0.4 hectares per person of arable land are needed at present productivity. The curve of land needed thus reflects the population growth curve. The light line after 1970 shows the projected need for land, assuming that world population continues to grow at its present rate. Arable land available decreases because arable land is removed for urban-industrial use as population grows. The dotted curves show land needed if present productivity is doubled or quadrupled.

The lower curve in figure 10 shows the amount of land needed to feed the growing world population, assuming that the present world average of 0.4 hectares per person is sufficient. (To feed the entire world population at present US standards, 0.9 hectares per person would be required.) The upper curve in figure 10 shows the actual amount of arable land available over time. This line slopes downward because each additional person requires a certain amount of land (0.08 hectares per person assumed here*) for housing, roads, waste disposal, power lines, and other uses that essentially "pave" arable land and make it unusable for food production. Land loss through erosion is not shown here, but it is by no means negligible. Figure 10 shows that, even with the optimistic assumption that all possible land is utilized, there will still be a desperate land shortage before the year 2000 if per capita land requirements and population growth rates remain as they are today.

Figure 10 also illustrates some very important general facts about exponential growth within a limited space. First, it shows how one can move within a very few years from a situation of great abundance to one of great scarcity. There has been an overwhelming excess of potentially arable land for all of history, and now, within 30 years (or about one population doubling time), there may be a sudden and serious shortage. Like the owner of the lily pond in our example in chapter I, the human race may have very little time to react to a crisis resulting from exponential growth in a finite space.

A second lesson to be learned from figure 10 is that precise numerical assumptions about the limits of the earth are unimportant when viewed against the inexorable progress of exponential growth. We might assume, for example, that *no* arable land is taken for cities, roads, or other nonagricultural uses. In that case, the land available is constant, as shown by the horizontal dashed line. The point at which the two curves cross is delayed by about 10 years. Or we can suppose that it is possible to double, or even quadruple, the productivity of the land through advances in agricultural technology and in-

* Aerial surveys of forty-four counties in the western United States from 1950 to 1960 indicate that built-on land ranged from .008 to .174 hectares per person.[9]

vestments in capital, such as tractors, fertilizer, and irrigation systems. The effects of two different assumptions about increased productivity are shown by the dotted lines in figure 10. Each doubling of productivity gains about 30 years, or less than one population doubling time.

Of course, society will not be suddenly surprised by the "crisis point" at which the amount of land needed becomes greater than that available. Symptoms of the crisis will begin to appear long before the crisis point is reached. Food prices will rise so high that some people will starve; others will be forced to decrease the effective amount of land they use and shift to lower quality diets. These symptoms are already apparent in many parts of the world. Although only half the land shown in figure 10 is now under cultivation, perhaps 10 to 20 million deaths each year can be attributed directly or indirectly to malnutrition.[10]

There is no question that many of these deaths are due to the world's social limitations rather than its physical ones. Yet there is clearly a link between these two kinds of limitations in the food-producing system. If good fertile land were still easily reached and brought under cultivation, there would be no economic barrier to feeding the hungry, and no difficult social choices to make. The best half of the world's potentially arable land is already cultivated, however, and opening new land is already so costly that society has judged it "uneconomic." This is a social problem exacerbated by a physical limitation.

Even if society did decide to pay the necessary costs to gain new land or to increase productivity of the land already cultivated, figure 10 shows how quickly rising population would bring about another "crisis point." And each successive crisis point will cost more to overcome. Each doubling of yield from the land will be more expensive than the last one. We might call this phenomenon the law of increasing costs. The best and most sobering example of that law comes from an assessment of the cost of past agricultural gains. To achieve a 34 percent increase in world food production from 1951 to 1966, agriculturalists increased yearly expenditures on tractors by 63 percent, annual investment in nitrate fertilizers by 146 percent, and annual use of pesticides by 300 percent.[11] The next 34 percent increase will require even greater inputs of capital and resources.

How many people can be fed on this earth? There is, of course, no simple answer to this question. The answer depends on the choices society makes among various available alternatives. There is a direct trade-off between producing more food and producing other goods and services needed or desired by mankind. The demand for these other goods and services is also increasing as population grows, and therefore the trade-off becomes continuously more apparent and more difficult to resolve. Even if the choice were consistently to produce food as the first priority, however, continued population growth and the law of increasing costs could rapidly drive the system to the point where all available resources were devoted to producing food, leaving no further possibility of expansion.

In this section we have discussed only one possible limit to food production—arable land. There are other possible limits, but space does not permit us to discuss them in detail here. The most obvious one, second in importance only to land, is the availability of fresh water. There is an upper limit to the fresh water runoff from the land areas of the earth each year, and there is also an exponentially increasing demand for that water. We could draw a graph exactly analogous to figure 10 to show the approach of the increasing demand curve for water to the constant average supply. In some areas of the world, this limit will be reached long before the land limit becomes apparent.

It is also possible to avoid or extend these limits by technological advances that remove dependence on the land (synthetic food) or that create new sources of fresh water (desalinization of sea water). We shall discuss such innovations further in chapter IV. For the moment it is sufficient to recognize that no new technology is spontaneous or without cost. The factories and raw materials to produce synthetic food, the equipment and energy to purify sea water must all come from the physical world system.

The exponential growth of *demand* for food results directly from the positive feedback loop that is now determining the growth of human population. The *supply* of food to be expected in the future is dependent on land and fresh water and also on agricultural capital, which depends in turn on the other dominant positive feedback loop in the system—the capital investment loop. Opening new land, farming the sea, or expanding use of fertilizers and pesticides will require an increase of the capital stock devoted to food production. The resources that permit growth of that capital stock tend not to be renewable resources, like land or water, but nonrenewable resources, like fuels or metals. Thus the expansion of food production in the future is very much dependent on the availability of nonrenewable resources. Are there limits to the earth's supply of these resources?

NONRENEWABLE RESOURCES

Even taking into account such economic factors as increased prices with decreasing availability, it would appear at present that the quantities of platinum, gold, zinc, and lead are not sufficient to meet demands. At the present rate of expansion . . . silver, tin, and uranium may be in short supply even at higher prices by the turn of the century. By the year 2050, several more minerals may be exhausted if the current rate of consumption continues.

Despite spectacular recent discoveries, there are only a limited number of places left to search for most minerals. Geologists disagree about the prospects for finding large, new, rich ore deposits. Reliance on such discoveries would seem unwise in the long term.[12]

Table 4 lists some of the more important mineral and fuel resources, the vital raw materials for today's major industrial processes. The number following each resource in column 3 is the static reserve index, or the number of years present known reserves of that resource (listed in column 2) will last at the *current* rate of usage. This static index is the measure normally used to express future resource availability. Underlying the static index are several assumptions, one of which is that the usage rate will remain constant.

But column 4 in table 4 shows that the world usage rate of every natural resource is growing exponentially. For many resources the usage rate is growing even faster than the population, indicating both that more people are consuming resources each year and also that the average consumption per person is increasing each year. In other words, the exponential growth curve of resource consumption is driven by both the positive feedback loops of population growth and of capital growth.

We have already seen in figure 10 that an exponential increase in land use can very quickly run up against the fixed amount of land available. An exponential increase in resource consumption can rapidly diminish a fixed store of resources in the same way. Figure 11, which is similar to figure 10, illus-

Table 4 NONRENEWABLE NATURAL RESOURCES

1	2	3	4			5	6
Resource	*Known Global Reserves* [a]	*Static Index (years)* [b]	*Projected Rate of Growth (% per Year)* [c]			*Exponential Index (years)* [d]	*Exponential Index Calculated Using 5 Times Known Reserves (years)* [e]
			High	*Av.*	*Low*		
Aluminum	1.17×10^9 tons [j]	100	7.7	6.4	5.1	31	55
Chromium	7.75×10^8 tons	420	3.3	2.6	2.0	95	154
Coal	5×10^{12} tons	2300	5.3	4.1	3.0 [k]	111	150
Cobalt	4.8×10^9 lbs	110	2.0	1.5	1.0	60	148
Copper	308×10^6 tons	36	5.8	4.6	3.4	21	48
Gold	353×10^6 troy oz	11	4.8	4.1	3.4 [l]	9	29
Iron	1×10^{11} tons	240	2.3	1.8	1.3	93	173
Lead	91×10^6 tons	26	2.4	2.0	1.7	21	64
Manganese	8×10^8 tons	97	3.5	2.9	2.4	46	94
Mercury	3.34×10^6 flasks	13	3.1	2.6	2.2	13	41

7	8	9	10
Countries or Areas with Highest Reserves (% of world total)[f]	*Prime Producers (% of world total)*[g]	*Prime Consumers (% of world total)*[h]	*US Consumption as % of World Total*[i]
Australia (33) Guinea (20) Jamaica (10)	Jamaica (19) Surinam (12)	US (42) USSR (12)	42
Rep. of S. Africa (75)	USSR (30) Turkey (10)		19
US (32) USSR-China (53)	USSR (20) US (24)		22
Rep. of Congo (31) Zambia (16)	Rep. of Congo (51)		32
US (28) Chile (19)	US (20) USSR (15) Zambia (13)	US (33) USSR (13) Japan (11)	33
Rep. of S. Africa (40)	Rep. of S. Africa (77) Canada (6)		26
USSR (33) S. Am. (18) Canada (14)	USSR (25) US (14)	US (28) USSR (24) W. Germany (7)	28
US (39)	USSR (13) Australia (13) Canada (11)	US (25) USSR (13) W. Germany (11)	25
Rep. of S. Africa (38) USSR (25)	USSR (34) Brazil (13) Rep. of S. Africa (13)		14
Spain (30) Italy (21)	Spain (22) Italy (21) USSR (18)		24

1	2	3	4			5	6
Resource	*Known Global Reserves* [a]	*Static Index (years)* [b]	*Projected Rate of Growth (% per Year)* [c]			*Exponential Index (years)* [d]	*Exponential Index Calculated Using 5 Times Known Reserves (years)*
			High	*Av.*	*Low*		
Molybdenum	10.8×10^9 lbs	79	5.0	4.5	4.0	34	65
Natural Gas	1.14×10^{15} cu ft	38	5.5	4.7	3.9	22	49
Nickel	147×10^9 lbs	150	4.0	3.4	2.8	53	96
Petroleum	455×10^9 bbls	31	4.9	3.9	2.9	20	50
Platinum Group [m]	429×10^6 troy oz	130	4.5	3.8	3.1	47	85
Silver	5.5×10^9 troy oz	16	4.0	2.7	1.5	13	42
Tin	4.3×10^6 lg tons	17	2.3	1.1	0	15	61
Tungsten	2.9×10^9 lbs	40	2.9	2.5	2.1	28	72
Zinc	123×10^6 tons	23	3.3	2.9	2.5	18	50

7	8	9	10
Countries or Areas with Highest Reserves (% of world total)[f]	*Prime Producers (% of world total)*[g]	*Prime Consumers (% of world total)*[h]	*US Consumption as % of World Total*[i]
US (58) USSR (20)	US (64) Canada (14)		40
US (25) USSR (13)	US (58) USSR (18)		63
Cuba (25) New Caledonia (22) USSR (14) Canada (14)	Canada (42) New Caledonia (28) USSR (16)		38
Saudi Arabia (17) Kuwait (15)	US (23) USSR (16)	US (33) USSR (12) Japan (6)	33
Rep. of S. Africa (47) USSR (47)	USSR (59)		31
Communist Countries (36) US (24)	Canada (20) Mexico (17) Peru (16)	US (26) W. Germany (11)	26
Thailand (33) Malaysia (14)	Malaysia (41) Bolivia (16) Thailand (13)	US (24) Japan (14)	24
China (73)	China (25) USSR (19) US (14)		22
US (27) Canada (20)	Canada (23) USSR (11) US (8)	US (26) Japan (13) USSR (11)	26

[a] SOURCE: US Bureau of Mines, *Mineral Facts and Problems, 1970* (Washington, DC: Government Printing Office, 1970).

[b] The number of years known global reserves will last at current global consumption. Calculated by dividing known reserves (column 2) by the current annual consumption (US Bureau of Mines, *Mineral Facts and Problems, 1970*).

[c] SOURCE: US Bureau of Mines, *Mineral Facts and Problems, 1970.*

[d] The number of years known global reserves will last with consumption growing exponentially at the average annual rate of growth. Calculated by the formula

$$\text{exponential index} = \frac{\ln((r \cdot s) + 1)}{r}$$

where r = average rate of growth from column 4
s = static index from column 3.

[e] The number of years that five times known global reserves will last with consumption growing exponentially at the average annual rate of growth. Calculated from the above formula with 5s in place of s.

[f] SOURCE: US Bureau of Mines, *Mineral Facts and Problems, 1970.*

[g] SOURCE: UN Department of Economic and Social Affairs, *Statistical Yearbook 1969* (New York: United Nations, 1970).

[h] SOURCES: *Yearbook of the American Bureau of Metal Statistics 1970* (York, Pa.: Maple Press, 1970).
World Petroleum Report (New York: Mona Palmer Publishing, 1968).
UN Economic Commission for Europe, *The World Market for Iron Ore* (New York: United Nations, 1968).
US Bureau of Mines, *Mineral Facts and Problems, 1970.*

[i] SOURCE: US Bureau of Mines, *Mineral Facts and Problems, 1970.*

[j] Bauxite expressed in aluminum equivalent.

[k] US Bureau of Mines contingency forecasts, based on assumptions that coal will be used to synthesize gas and liquid fuels.

[l] Includes US Bureau of Mines estimates of gold demand for hoarding.

[m] The platinum group metals are platinum, palladium, iridium, osmium, rhodium, and ruthenium.

ADDITIONAL SOURCES:
P. T. Flawn, *Mineral Resources* (Skokie, Ill.: Rand McNally, 1966).
Metal Statistics (Somerset, NJ: American Metal Market Company, 1970).
US Bureau of Mines, *Commodity Data Summary* (Washington, DC: Government Printing Office, January 1971).

trates the effect of exponentially increasing consumption of a given initial amount of a nonrenewable resource. The example in this case is chromium ore, chosen because it has one of the longest static reserve indices of all the resources listed in table 4. We could draw a similar graph for each of the resources listed in the table. The time scales for the resources would vary, but the general shape of the curves would be the same.

The world's known reserves of chromium are about 775 million metric tons, of which about 1.85 million metric tons are mined annually at present.[13] Thus, at the current rate of use, the known reserves would last about 420 years. The dashed line in figure 11 illustrates the linear depletion of chromium reserves that would be expected under the assumption of constant use. The actual world consumption of chromium is increasing, however, at the rate of 2.6 percent annually.[13] The curved solid lines in figure 11 show how that growth rate, if it continues, will deplete the resource stock, not in 420 years, as the linear assumption indicates, but in just 95 years. If we suppose that reserves yet undiscovered could increase present known reserves by a factor of five, as shown by the dotted line, this fivefold increase would extend the lifetime of the reserves only from 95 to 154 years. Even if it were possible from 1970 onward to recycle 100 percent of the chromium (the horizontal line) so that none of the initial reserves were lost, the demand would exceed the supply in 235 years.

Figure 11 shows that under conditions of exponential growth in resource consumption, the static reserve index (420 years for chromium) is a rather misleading measure of resource availability. We might define a new index, an "exponential reserve index," which gives the probable lifetime of each resource, assuming that the current growth rate in consumption will

Figure 11 CHROMIUM RESERVES

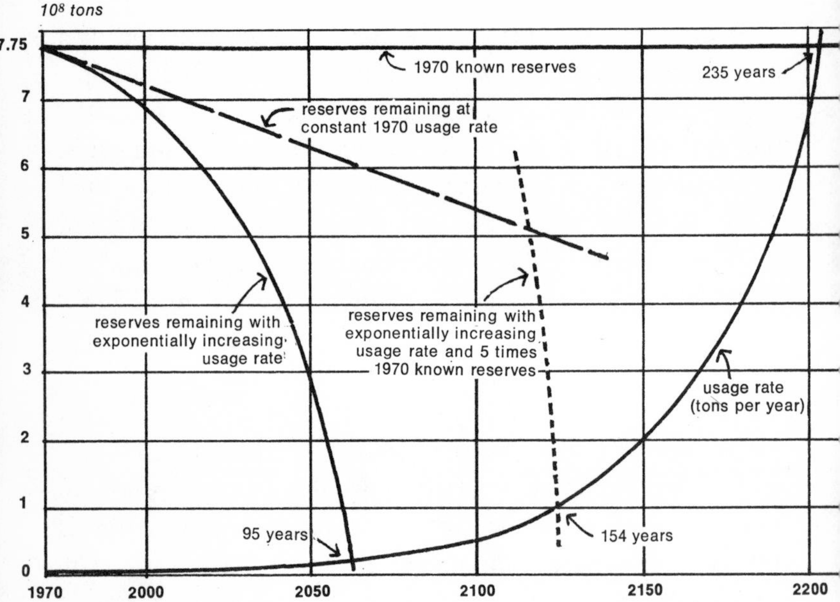

The lifetime of known chromium reserves depends on the future usage rate of chromium. If usage remains constant, reserves will be depleted linearly (dashed line) and will last 420 years. If usage increases exponentially at its present growth rate of 2.6 percent per year, reserves will be depleted in just 95 years. If actual reserves are five times present proven reserves, chromium ore will be available for 154 years (dotted line), assuming exponential growth in usage. Even if all chromium is perfectly recycled, starting in 1970, exponentially growing demand will exceed the supply after 235 years (horizontal line).

continue. We have included this index in column 5 of table 4. We have also calculated an exponential index on the assumption that our present known reserves of each resource can be expanded fivefold by new discoveries. This index is shown in column 6. The effect of exponential growth is to reduce the probable period of availability of aluminum, for example, from 100 years to 31 years (55 years with a fivefold increase in reserves). Copper, with a 36-year lifetime at the present usage rate, would actually last only 21 years at the present rate of growth, and 48 years if reserves are multiplied by five. It is clear that the present exponentially growing usage rates greatly diminish the length of time that wide-scale economic growth can be based on these raw materials.

Of course the actual nonrenewable resource availability in the next few decades will be determined by factors much more complicated than can be expressed by either the simple static reserve index or the exponential reserve index. We have studied this problem with a detailed model that takes into account the many interrelationships among such factors as varying grades of ore, production costs, new mining technology, the elasticity of consumer demand, and substitution of other resources.* Illustrations of the general conclusions of this model follow.

Figure 12 is a computer plot indicating the future availability of a resource with a 400-year static reserve index in the year 1970, such as chromium. The horizontal axis is time in years; the vertical axis indicates several quantities, including the amount of reserves remaining (labeled RESERVES), the amount used each year (USAGE RATE), the extraction cost per unit of resource (ACTUAL COST), the advance of mining and processing technology (indicated by a T), and the fraction of original use of the resource that has been shifted to a substitute resource (F).

At first the annual consumption of chromium grows exponentially, and the stock of the resource is rapidly depleted. The price of chromium remains low and constant because new developments in mining technology allow efficient use of lower

---

* A more complete description of this model is presented in the paper by William W. Behrens III listed in the appendix.

Figure 12 CHROMIUM AVAILABILITY

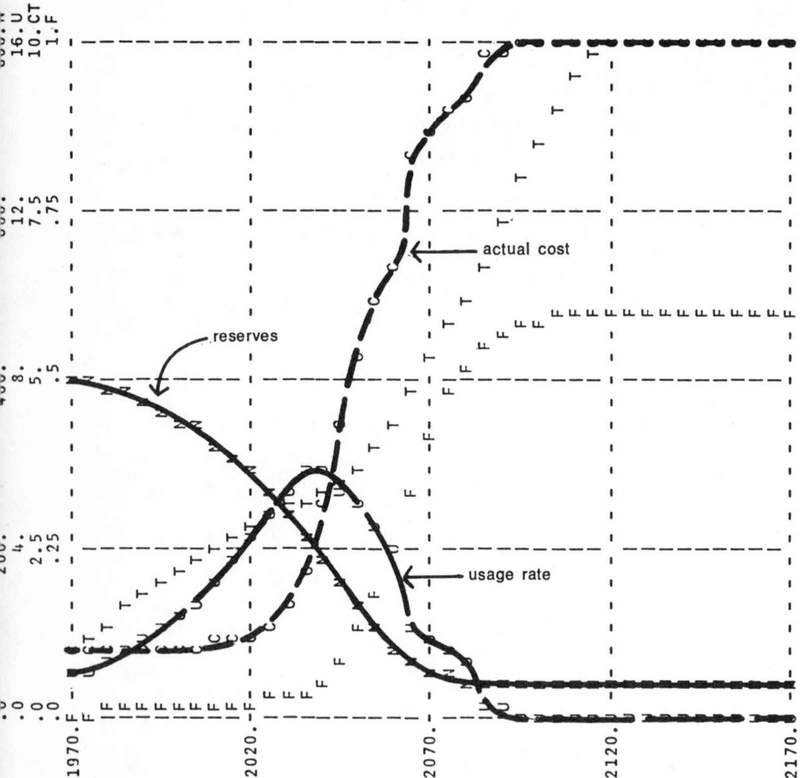

This figure presents a computer calculation of the economic factors in the availability of a resource (chromium) with a 400-year static reserve index. Exponential growth in consumption is eventually stopped by rising costs as initial reserves are depleted, even though the technology of extraction and processing is also increasing exponentially. The usage rate falls to zero after 125 years, at which point 60 percent of the original uses have been substituted by another resource.

SOURCE: William W. Behrens III, "The Dynamics of Natural Resource Utilization," in Dennis L. Meadows and Donella H. Meadows, *Toward Global Equilibrium* (Cambridge, Mass.: Wright-Allen Press, 1973).

and lower grades of ore. As demand continues to increase, however, the advance of technology is not fast enough to counteract the rising costs of discovery, extraction, processing,

Figure 13 CHROMIUM AVAILABILITY WITH DOUBLE THE KNOWN RESERVES

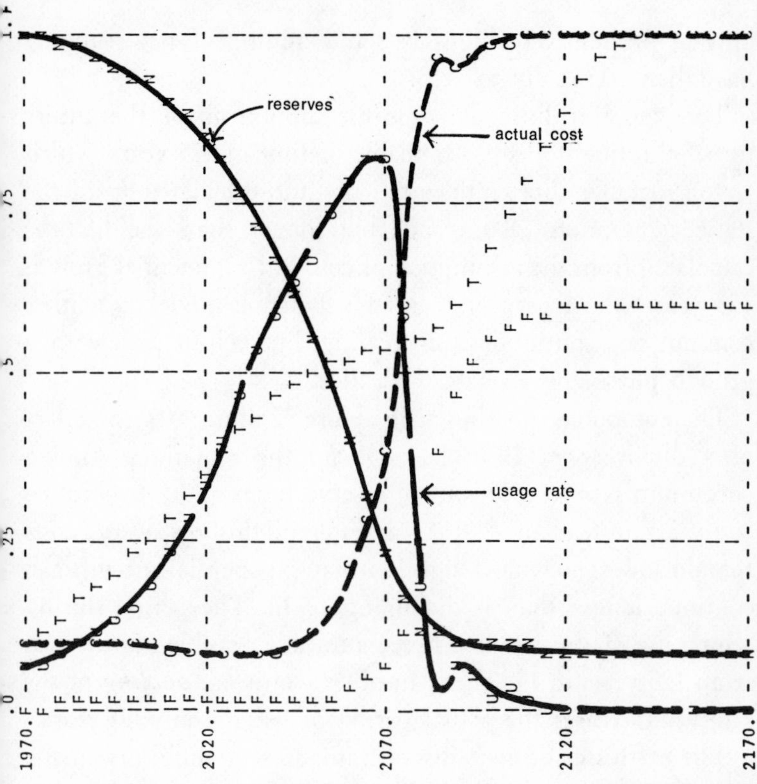

If a discovery in 1970 doubles the known reserves of the resource (static reserve index 800 years), exponential growth in the usage rate is prolonged, and the usage rate reaches a high value. Reserves are depleted very rapidly during the peak in usage rate, however. Because of this rapid depletion, the effect of doubling the reserves is not to double the resource lifetime, but merely to extend it from 125 to 145 years.

SOURCE: William W. Behrens, III, "The Dynamics of Natural Resource Utilization."

and distribution. Price begins to rise, slowly at first and then very rapidly. The higher price causes consumers to use chromium more efficiently and to substitute other metals for chromium whenever possible. After 125 years, the remaining chromium, about 5 percent of the original supply, is available only at prohibitively high cost, and mining of new supplies has fallen essentially to zero.

This more realistic dynamic assumption about the future use of chromium yields a probable lifetime of 125 years, which is considerably shorter than the lifetime calculated from the static assumption (400 years), but longer than the lifetime calculated from the assumption of constant exponential growth (95 years). The usage rate in the dynamic model is neither constant nor continuously increasing, but bell-shaped, with a growth phase and a phase of decline.

The computer run shown in figure 13 illustrates the effect of a discovery in 1970 that *doubles* the remaining known chromium reserves. The static reserve index in 1970 becomes 800 years instead of 400. As a result of this discovery, costs remain low somewhat longer, so that exponential growth can continue longer than it did in figure 12. The period during which use of the resource is economically feasible is increased from 125 years to 145 years. In other words, a *doubling* of the reserves increases the actual period of use by only 20 years.

The earth's crust contains vast amounts of those raw materials which man has learned to mine and to transform into useful things. However vast those amounts may be, they are not infinite. Now that we have seen how suddenly an exponentially growing quantity approaches a fixed upper limit, the following statement should not come as a surprise. *Given present resource consumption rates and the projected increase in these rates, the great majority of the currently important nonrenewable resources will be extremely costly 100 years from now.* The above statement remains true regardless of the most optimistic assumptions about undiscovered reserves, technological advances, substitution, or recycling, as long as the demand for resources continues to grow exponentially. The prices of those resources with the shortest static reserve indices have already begun to increase. The price of mercury, for example, has gone up 500 percent in the last 20 years; the price of lead has increased 300 percent in the last 30 years.[14]

The simple conclusions we have drawn by considering total world reserves of resources are further complicated by the fact that neither resource reserves nor resource consumption are distributed evenly about the globe. The last four columns of table 4 show clearly that the industrialized, consuming countries are heavily dependent on a network of international agreements with the producing countries for the supply of raw materials essential to their industrial base. Added to the difficult economic question of the fate of various industries as resource after resource becomes prohibitively expensive is the imponderable political question of the relationships between producer and consumer nations as the remaining resources become concentrated in more limited geographical areas. Recent nationalization of South American mines and successful Middle Eastern pressures to raise oil prices suggest that the political question may arise long before the ultimate economic one.

Are there enough resources to allow the economic development of the 7 billion people expected by the year 2000 to a reasonably high standard of living? Once again the answer must be a conditional one. It depends on how the major resource-consuming societies handle some important decisions ahead. They might continue to increase resource consumption according to the present pattern. They might learn to reclaim and recycle discarded materials. They might develop new designs to increase the durability of products made from scarce resources. They might encourage social and economic patterns that would satisfy the needs of a person while minimizing, rather than maximizing, the irreplaceable substances he possesses and disperses.

All of these possible courses involve trade-offs. The trade-offs are particularly difficult in this case because they involve choosing between present benefits and future benefits. In order to guarantee the availability of adequate resources in the future, policies must be adopted that will decrease resource use in the present. Most of these policies operate by raising resource costs. Recycling and better product design are expensive; in most parts of the world today they are considered "uneconomic." Even if they were effectively instituted, however, as long as the driving feedback loops of population and industrial growth continue to generate more people and a higher resource demand per capita, the system is being pushed toward its limit—the depletion of the earth's nonrenewable resources.

What happens to the metals and fuels extracted from the earth after they have been used and discarded? In one sense they are never lost. Their constituent atoms are rearranged and eventually dispersed in a diluted and unusable form into the air, the soil, and the waters of our planet. The natural ecological systems can absorb many of the effluents of human activity and reprocess them into substances that are usable by, or at least harmless to, other forms of life. When any effluent is released on a large enough scale, however, the natural absorptive mechanisms can become saturated. The wastes of human civilization can build up in the environment until they become visible, annoying, and even harmful. Mercury in ocean fish, lead particles in city air, mountains of urban trash, oil slicks on beaches—these are the results of the increasing flow of resources into and out of man's hands. It is little wonder, then, that another exponentially increasing quantity in the world system is pollution.

POLLUTION

Many people . . . are concluding on the basis of mounting and reasonably objective evidence that the length of life of the biosphere as an inhabitable region for organisms is to be measured in decades rather than in hundreds of millions of years. This is entirely the fault of our own species.[15]

Man's concern for the effect of his activities on the natural environment is only very recent. Scientific attempts to measure this effect are even more recent and still very incomplete. We are certainly not able, at this time, to come to any final conclusion about the earth's capacity to absorb pollution. We can, however, make four basic points in this section, which illustrate, from a dynamic, global perspective, how difficult it will be to understand and control the future state of our ecological systems. These points are:

1. The few kinds of pollution that actually have been measured over time seem to be increasing exponentially.
2. We have almost no knowledge about where the upper limits to these pollution growth curves might be.
3. The presence of natural delays in ecological processes increases the probability of underestimating the control measures necessary, and therefore of inadvertently reaching those upper limits.
4. Many pollutants are globally distributed; their harmful effects appear long distances from their points of generation.

It is not possible to illustrate each of these four points for each type of pollutant, both because of the space limitations

Figure 14 ENERGY CONSUMPTION AND GNP PER CAPITA

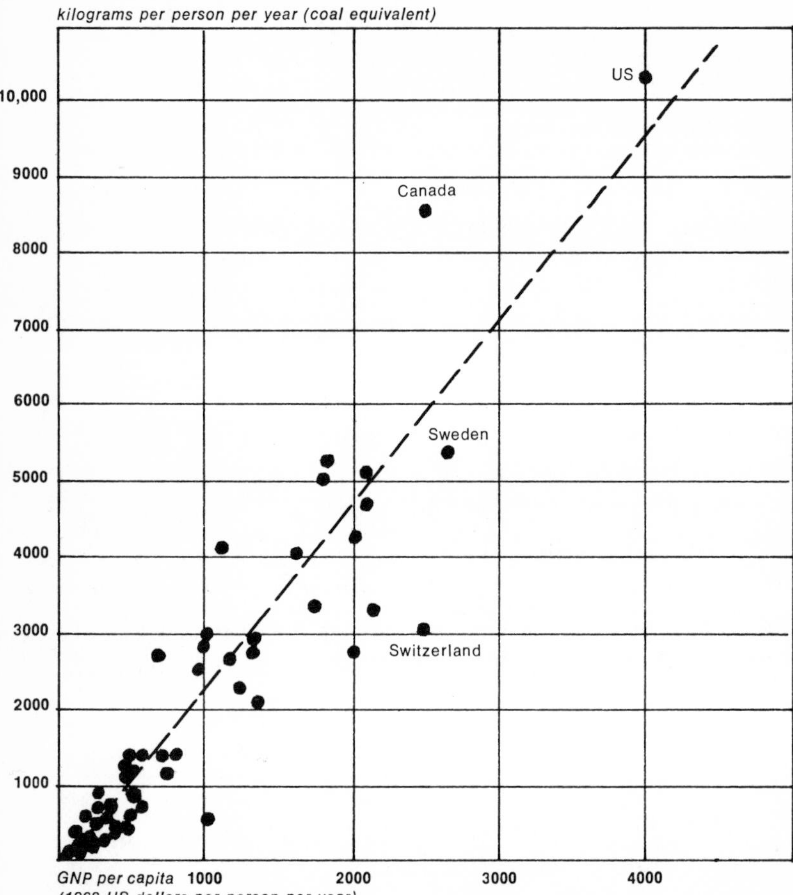

Although the nations of the world consume greatly varying amounts of energy per capita, energy consumption correlates fairly well with total output per capita (GNP per capita). The relationship is generally linear, with the scattering of points due to differences in climate, local fuel prices, and emphasis on heavy industry.

SOURCES: Energy consumption from UN Department of Economic and Social Affairs, *Statistical Yearbook 1969* (New York: United Nations, 1970). GNP per capita from *World Bank Atlas* (Washington, DC: International Bank for Reconstruction and Development, 1970).

of this book and because of the limitations of available data. Therefore we shall discuss each point using as examples those pollutants which have been most completely studied to date. It is not necessarily true that the pollutants mentioned here are the ones of greatest concern (although they are all of some concern). They are, rather, the ones we understand best.

Exponentially increasing pollution

Virtually every pollutant that has been measured as a function of time appears to be increasing exponentially. The rates of increase of the various examples shown below vary greatly, but most are growing faster than the population. Some pollutants are obviously directly related to population growth (or agricultural activity, which is related to population growth). Others are more closely related to the growth of industry and advances in technology. Most pollutants in the complicated world system are influenced in some way by *both* the population and the industrialization positive feedback loops.

Let us begin by looking at the pollutants related to mankind's increasing use of energy. The process of economic development is in effect the process of utilizing more energy to increase the productivity and efficiency of human labor. In fact, one of the best indications of the wealth of a human population is the amount of energy it consumes per person (see figure 14). Per capita energy consumption in the world is increasing at a rate of 1.3 percent per year,[16] which means a total increase, including population growth, of 3.4 percent per year.

At present about 97 percent of mankind's industrial energy production comes from fossil fuels (coal, oil, and natural gas).[17] When these fuels are burned, they release, among other

Figure 15 CARBON DIOXIDE CONCENTRATION IN THE ATMOSPHERE

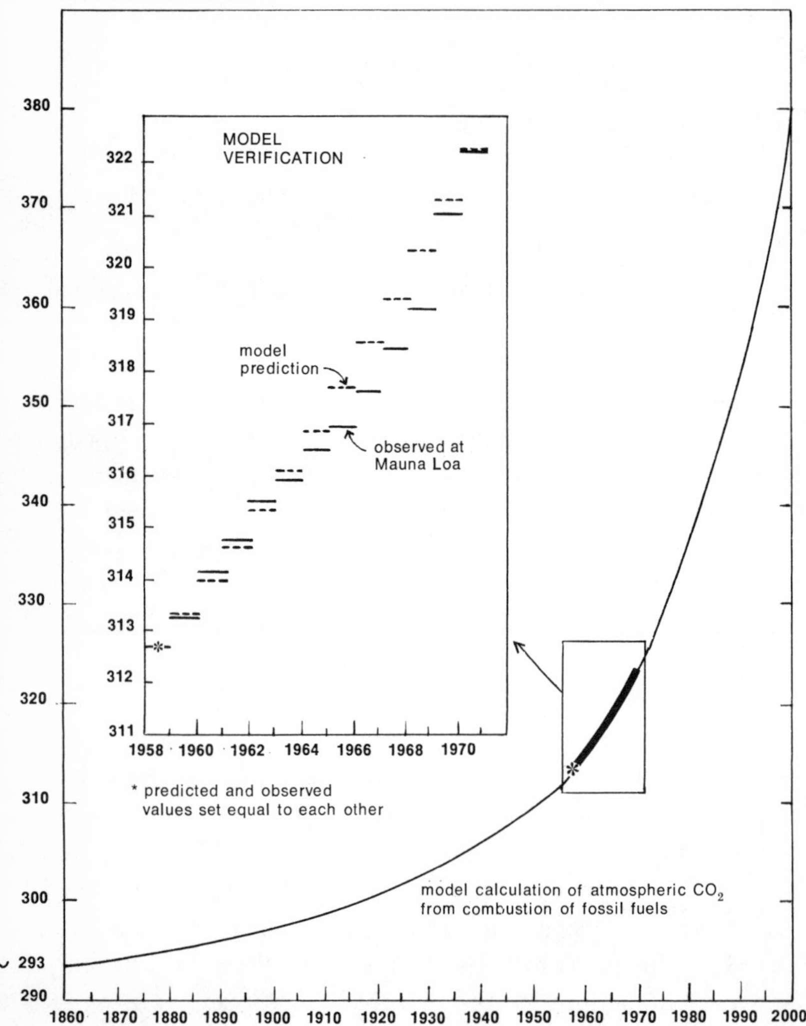

Atmospheric concentration of CO_2, observed since 1958 at Mauna Loa, Hawaii, has increased steadily. At present the increase averages about 1.5 part per million (ppm) each year. Calculations including the known exchanges of CO_2 between atmosphere, biosphere, and oceans predict that

the CO_2 concentration will reach 380 ppm by the year 2000, an increase of nearly 30 percent of the probable value in 1860. The source of this exponential increase in atmospheric CO_2 is man's increasing combustion of fossil fuels.

SOURCE: Lester Machta, "The Role of the Oceans and Biosphere in the Carbon Dioxide Cycle." Paper presented at Nobel Symposium 20 "The Changing Chemistry of the Oceans," Göteborg, Sweden, August 1971.

substances, carbon dioxide (CO_2) into the atmosphere. Currently about 20 billion tons of CO_2 are being released from fossil fuel combustion each year.[18] As figure 15 shows, the measured amount of CO_2 in the atmosphere is increasing exponentially, apparently at a rate of about 0.2 percent per year. Only about one half of the CO_2 released from burning fossil fuels has actually appeared in the atmosphere—the other half has apparently been absorbed, mainly by the surface water of the oceans.[19]

If man's energy needs are someday supplied by nuclear power instead of fossil fuels, this increase in atmospheric CO_2 will eventually cease, one hopes before it has had any measurable ecological or climatological effect.

There is, however, another side-effect of energy use, which is independent of the fuel source. By the laws of thermodynamics, essentially all of the energy used by man must ultimately be dissipated as heat. If the energy source is something other than incident solar energy (e.g., fossil fuels or atomic energy), that heat will result in warming the atmosphere, either directly, or indirectly through radiation from water used for cooling purposes. Locally, waste heat or "thermal pollution" in streams causes disruption in the balance of aquatic life.[20] Atmospheric waste heat around cities causes the formation of urban "heat islands," within which many meteorological anomalies occur.[21] Thermal pollution may have serious climatic effects, worldwide, when it reaches some appre-

Figure 16 WASTE HEAT GENERATION IN THE LOS ANGELES BASIN

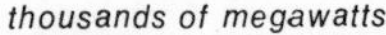

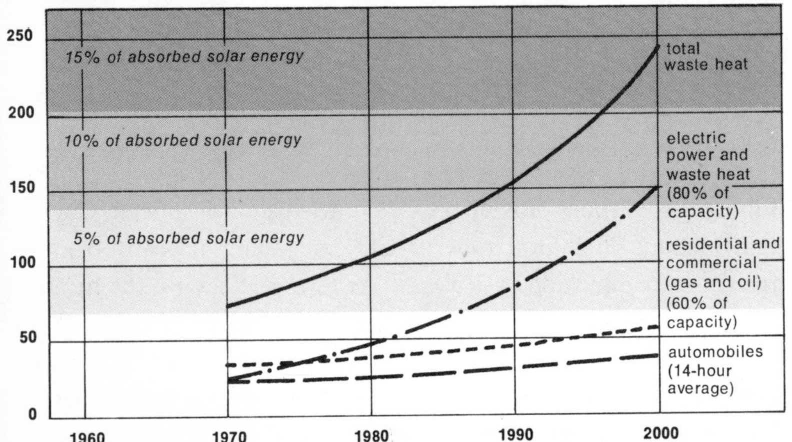

Waste heat released over the 4,000 square mile area of the Los Angeles basin currently amounts to about 5 percent of the total solar energy absorbed at the ground. At the present rate of growth, thermal release will reach 18 percent of incoming solar energy by the year 2000. This heat, the result of all energy generation and consumption processes, is already affecting the local climate.

SOURCE: L. Lees in *Man's Impact on the Global Environment,* Report of the Study of Critical Environmental Problems (Cambridge, Mass.: MIT Press, 1970).

ciable fraction of the energy normally absorbed by the earth from the sun.[22] In figure 16, the level of thermal pollution projected for one large city is shown as a fraction of incident solar energy.

Nuclear power will produce yet another kind of pollutant —radioactive wastes. Since nuclear power now provides only an insignificant fraction of the energy used by man, the possible environmental impact of the wastes released by nuclear reactors can only be surmised. Some idea may be gained, however, by the actual and expected releases of radioactive isotopes from the nuclear power plants being built today. A partial list of the expected annual discharge to the environment of a

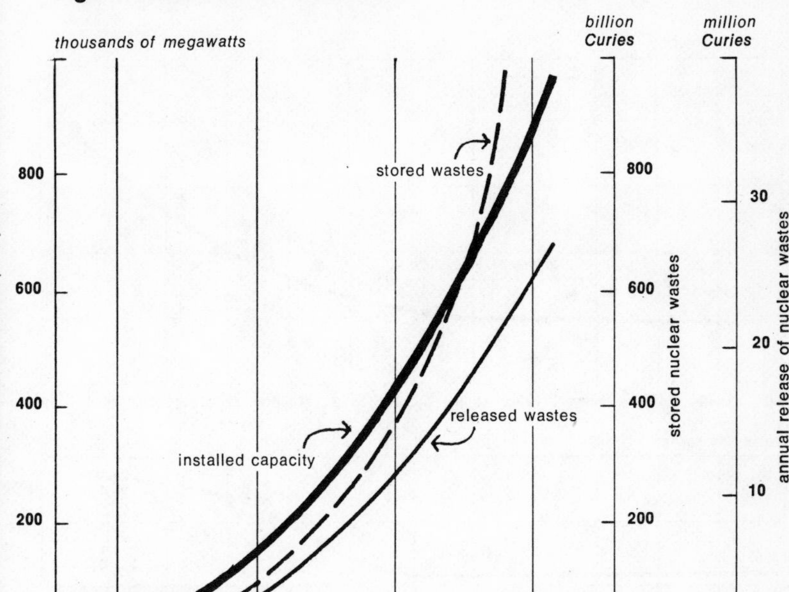

Installed nuclear generating capacity in the United States is expected to grow from 11 thousand megawatts in 1970 to more than 900 thousand megawatts in the year 2000. Total amount of stored nuclear wastes, radioactive by-products of the energy production, will probably exceed one thousand billion Curies by that year. Annual release of nuclear wastes, mostly in the form of krypton gas and tritium in cooling water, will reach 25 million Curies, if present release standards are still in effect.

SOURCES: Installed capacity to 1985 from US Atomic Energy Commission, *Forecast of Growth of Nuclear Power* (Washington, DC: Government Printing Office, 1971). Installed capacity to 2000 from Chauncey Starr, "Energy and Power," *Scientific American*, September 1971. Stored nuclear wastes from J. A. Snow, "Radioactive Waste from Reactors," *Scientist and Citizen* 9 (1967). Annual release of nuclear wastes calculated from specifications for 1.6 thousand megawatt plant in Calvert Cliffs, Maryland.

1.6 million kilowatt plant now under construction in the United States includes 42,800 Curies* of radioactive krypton

* A Curie is the radioactive equivalent of one gram of radium. This is such a large amount of radiation that environmental concentrations are usually expressed in microcuries (millionths of a Curie).

Figure 18 CHANGES IN CHEMICAL CHARACTERISTICS AND COMMERCIAL FISH PRODUCTION IN LAKE ONTARIO

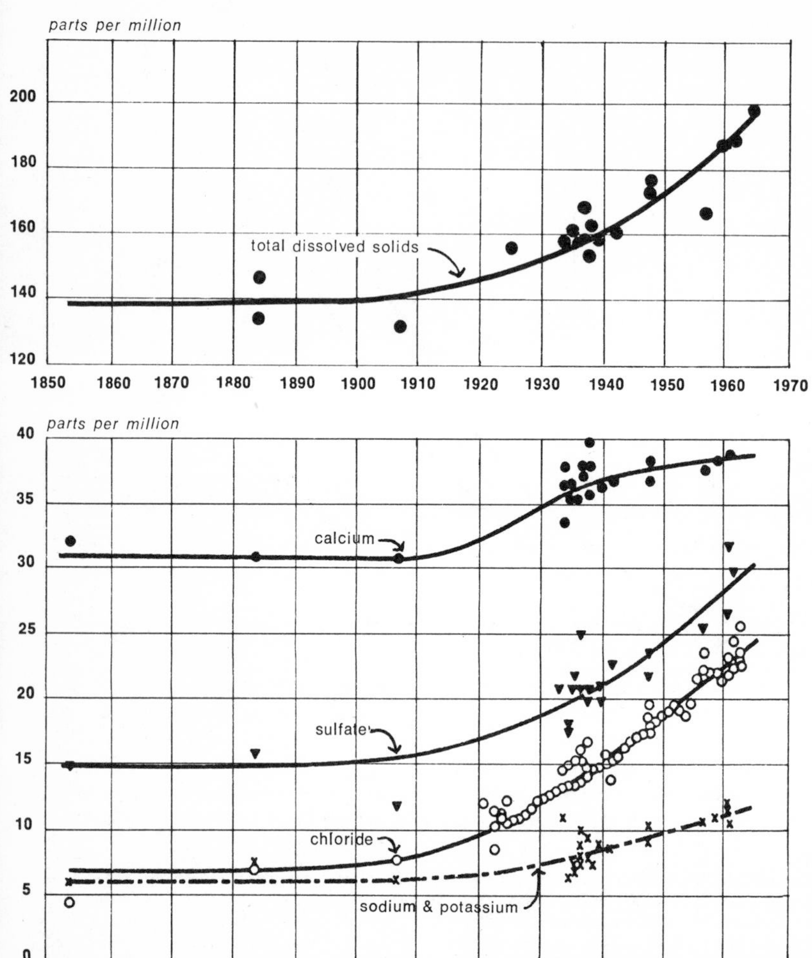

As a result of heavy dumping of municipal, industrial, and agricultural wastes into Lake Ontario, the concentrations of numerous salts have been rising exponentially. The chemical changes in the lake have resulted in severe declines in the catches of most commercially valuable fish. It should be noted that the plotting scale for fish catch is logarithmic, and thus the fish catch has decreased by factors of 100 to 1,000 for most species.

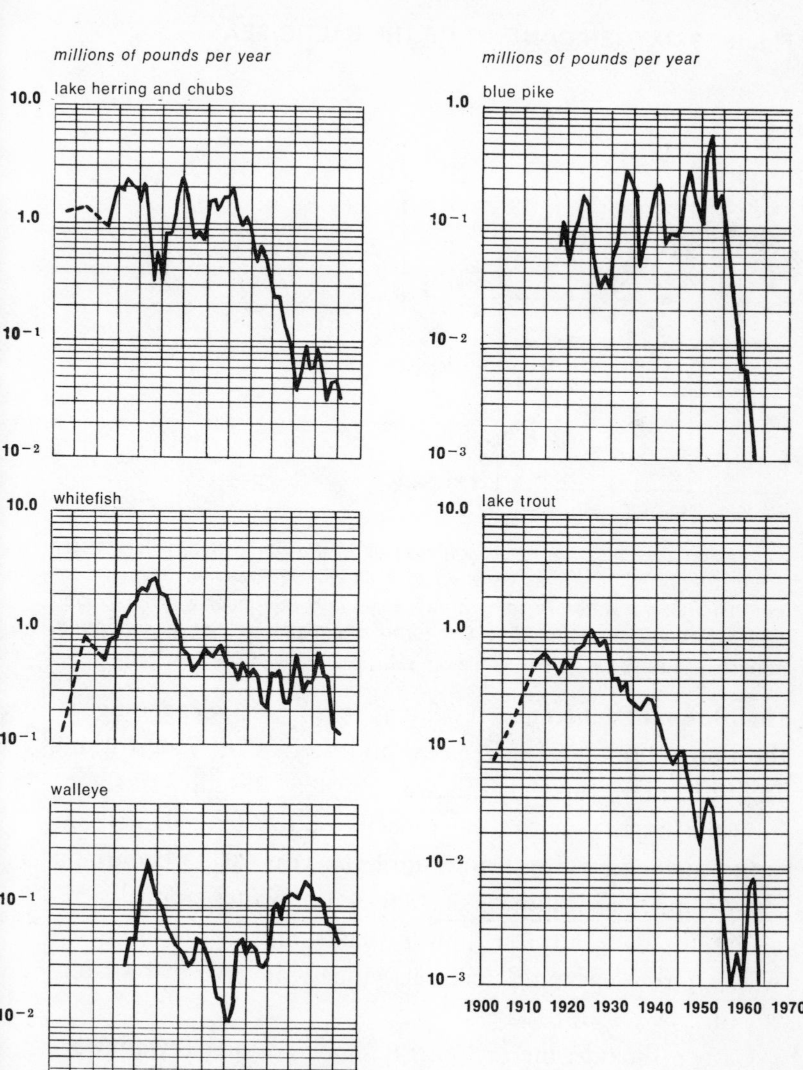

SOURCE: A. M. Beeton, *Statement on Pollution and Eutrophication of the Great Lakes,* The University of Wisconsin Center for Great Lakes Studies Special Report #11 (Milwaukee, Wisc.: University of Wisconsin, 1970).

Figure 19 OXYGEN CONTENT OF THE BALTIC SEA

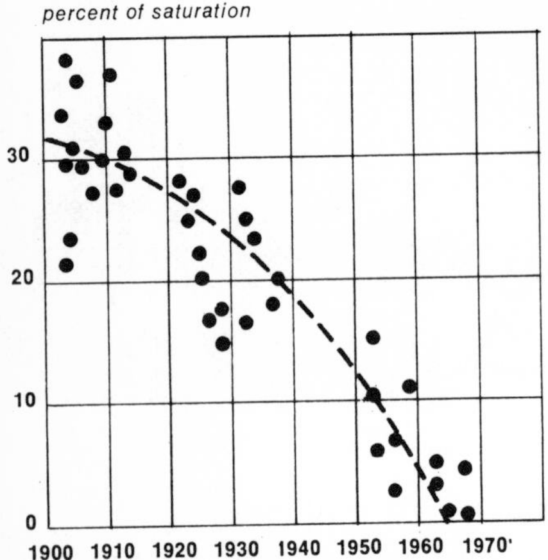

Increasing accumulation of organic wastes in the Baltic Sea, where water circulation is minimal, has resulted in a steadily decreasing oxygen concentration in the water. In some areas, especially in deeper waters, oxygen concentration is zero and almost no forms of aquatic life can be supported.

SOURCE: Stig H. Fonselius, "Stagnant Sea," *Environment*, July/August 1970.

(half-life ranging from a few hours to 9.4 years, depending on the isotope) in the stack gases, and 2,910 Curies of tritium (half-life 12.5 years) in the waste water.[23] Figure 17 shows how the nuclear generating capacity of the United States is expected to grow from now until the year 2000. The graph also includes an estimate of radioactive wastes annually released by these nuclear power plants and of accumulated wastes (from spent reactor fuels) that will have to be safely stored.

Carbon dioxide, thermal energy, and radioactive wastes are just three of the many disturbances man is inserting into the environment at an exponentially increasing rate. Other examples are shown in figures 18–21.

Figure 18 shows the chemical changes occurring in a large North American lake from accumulation of soluble industrial,

Figure 20 US MERCURY CONSUMPTION

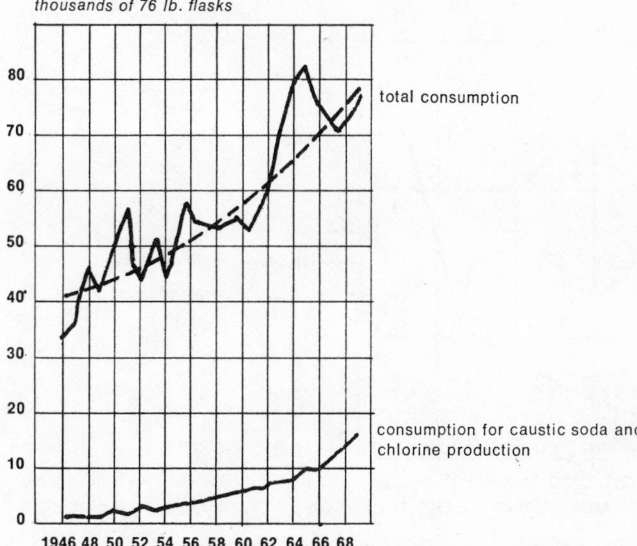

Mercury consumption in the United States shows an exponential trend, on which short-term market fluctuations are superimposed. A large part of the mercury is used for the production of caustic soda and chlorine. The chart does not include the rising amount of mercury released into the atmosphere from the combustion of fossil fuels.

SOURCE: Barry Commoner, Michael Carr, and Paul J. Stamler, "The Causes of Pollution," *Environment*, April 1971.

agricultural, and municipal wastes. The accompanying decrease in commercial fish production from the lake is also indicated. Figure 19 illustrates why the increase in organic wastes has such a catastrophic effect on fish life. The figure shows the amount of dissolved oxygen (which fish "breathe") in the Baltic Sea as a function of time. As increasing amounts of wastes enter the water and decay, the dissolved oxygen is depleted. In the case of some parts of the Baltic, the oxygen level has actually reached zero.

The toxic metals lead and mercury are released into waterways and into the atmosphere from automobiles, incinerators,

Figure 21 LEAD IN THE GREENLAND ICE CAP

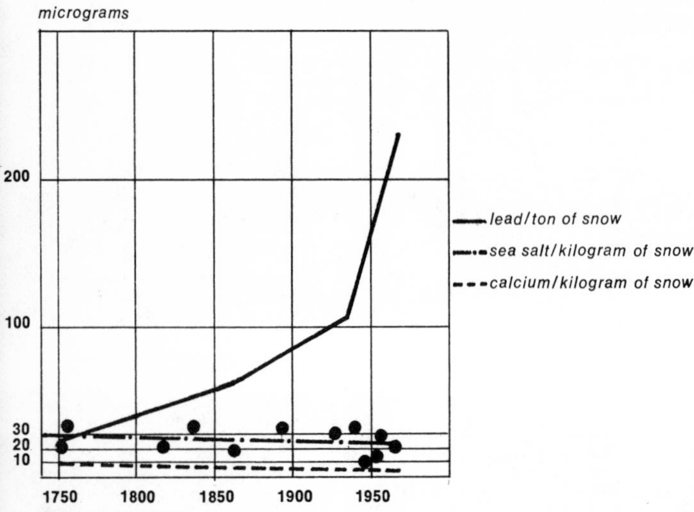

Deep samples of snow from the Greenland Ice Sheet show increasingly high deposits of lead over time. Concentrations of calcium and sea salt were also measured as a control. Presence of lead reflects increasing world industrial use of the metal, including direct release into the atmosphere from automobile exhausts.

SOURCE: C. C. Patterson and J. D. Salvia, "Lead in the Modern Environment—How Much is Natural?" *Scientist and Citizen,* April 1968.

industrial processes, and agricultural pesticides. Figure 20 shows the exponential increase in mercury consumption in the United States from 1946 to 1968. Only 18 percent of this mercury is captured and recycled after use.[24] An exponential increase in deposits of airborne lead has been detected by extraction of successively deeper samples from the Greenland ice cap, as shown in figure 21.

Unknown upper limits

All of these exponential curves of various kinds of pollution can be extrapolated into the future, as we have extrapolated land needs in figure 10 and resource use in figure 11. In both of these previous figures, the exponential growth curve eventually reached an upper limit—the total amount of arable land or of resources economically available in the earth. However, no upper bounds have been indicated for the exponential growth curves of pollutants in figures 15–21, because it is not known how much we can perturb the natural ecological balance of the earth without serious consequences. It is not known how much CO_2 or thermal pollution can be released without causing irreversible changes in the earth's climate, or how much radioactivity, lead, mercury, or pesticide can be absorbed by plants, fish, or human beings before the vital processes are severely interrupted.

Natural delays in ecological processes

This ignorance about the limits of the earth's ability to absorb pollutants should be reason enough for caution in the release of polluting substances. The danger of reaching those limits is especially great because there is typically a long delay between the release of a pollutant into the environment and the appearance of its negative effect on the ecosystem. The dynamic implications of such a delayed effect can be illustrated by the path of DDT through the environment after its use as an insecticide. The results presented below are taken from a detailed System Dynamics study* using the numerical constants appropriate to DDT. The general conclusion is applicable (with some change in the exact numbers involved) to all long-lived toxic substances, such as mercury, lead, cadmium, other pesticides, polychlorobiphenyl (PCB), and radioactive wastes.

---

* The study, by Jørgen Randers and Dennis L. Meadows, is listed in the appendix.

DDT is a man-made organic chemical released into the environment as a pesticide at a rate of about 100,000 tons annually.[25] After its application by spraying, part of it evaporates and is carried long distances in the air before it eventually precipitates back onto the land or into the ocean. In the ocean some of the DDT is taken up by plankton, some of the plankton are eaten by fish, and some of the fish are finally eaten by man. At each step in the process the DDT may be degraded into harmless substances, it may be released back into the ocean, or it may be concentrated in the tissues of living organisms. There is some time delay involved at each of these steps. All these possible pathways have been analyzed by a computer to produce the results seen in figure 22.

The DDT application rate shown in the figure follows the world application rate from 1940 to 1970. The graph shows what would happen if in 1970 the world DDT application rate began to decrease gradually until it reached zero in the year 2000. Because of the inherent delays in the system, the level of DDT in fish continues to rise for more than 10 years after DDT use starts declining, and the level in fish *does not come back down to the 1970 level until the year 1995*—more than two decades after the decision is made to reduce DDT application.

Whenever there is a long delay from the time of release of a pollutant to the time of its appearance in a harmful form, we know there will be an equally long delay from the time of *control* of that pollutant to the time when its harmful effect finally decreases. In other words, any pollution control system based on instituting controls only when some harm is already detected will probably guarantee that the problem will get much worse before it gets better. Systems of this sort are

Figure 22 DDT FLOWS IN THE ENVIRONMENT

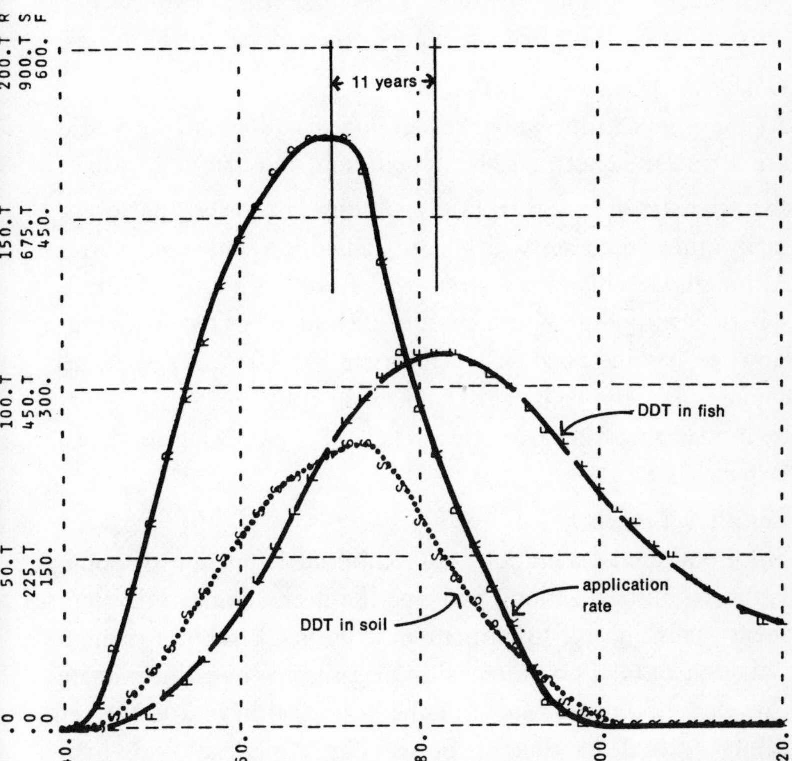

Calculation of the path of DDT through the environment shows the probable result if the world DDT application rate began to decline in 1970. The application rate shown is historically correct to 1970. DDT in soil peaks shortly after the application rate begins to decline, but DDT in fish continues to rise for 11 years and does not fall back to its 1970 level until 1995. DDT in fish-eating animals, such as birds and man, would show an even longer delay in responding to the decrease in application rate.

SOURCE: Jørgen Randers, "DDT Movement in the Global Environment," in Dennis L. Meadows and Donella H. Meadows, *Toward Global Equilibrium* (Cambridge, Mass.: Wright-Allen Press, 1973).

exceedingly difficult to control, because they require that present actions be based on results expected far in the future.

Global distribution of pollutants

At the present time only the developed nations of the world are seriously concerned about pollution. It is an unfortunate characteristic of many types of pollution, however, that eventually they become widely distributed around the world. Although Greenland is far removed from any source of atmospheric lead pollution, the amount of lead deposited in Greenland ice has increased 300 percent since 1940.[26] DDT has accumulated in the body fat of humans in every part of the globe, from Alaskan eskimos to city-dwellers of New Delhi, as shown in table 5.

Pollution Limits

Since pollution generation is a complicated function of population, industrialization, and specific technological developments, it is difficult to estimate exactly how fast the exponential curve of total pollution release is rising. We might estimate that if the 7 billion people of the year 2000 have a GNP per capita as high as that of present-day Americans, the total pollution load on the environment would be at least ten times its present value. Can the earth's natural systems support an intrusion of that magnitude? We have no idea. Some people believe that man has already so degraded the environment that irreversible damage has been done to large natural systems. We do not know the precise upper limit of the earth's ability to absorb any single kind of pollution, much less its ability to absorb the combination of all kinds of pollution. We do know however that there *is* an upper limit. It has already been surpassed in many local environments. The surest way to

Table 5 DDT IN BODY FAT

Population	*Year*	*Number in sample*	*Concentration of DDT and toxic breakdown products in body fat (parts per million)*
Alaska (Eskimos)	1960	20	3.0
Canada	1959–60	62	4.9
England	1961–62	131	2.2
England	1964	100	3.9
France	1961	10	5.2
Germany	1958–59	60	2.3
Hungary	1960	48	12.4
India (Delhi)	1964	67	26.0
Israel	1963–64	254	19.2
United States (Kentucky)	1942	10	.0
United States (Georgia, Kentucky, Arizona, Washington)	1961–62	130	12.7
United States (all areas)	1964	64	7.6

SOURCE: Wayland J. Hayes, Jr., "Monitoring Food and People for Pesticide Content," in *Scientific Aspects of Pest Control* (Washington, DC: National Academy of Sciences—National Research Council, 1966).

reach that upper limit globally is to increase exponentially both the number of people and the polluting activities of each person.

The trade-offs involved in the environmental sector of the world system are every bit as difficult to resolve as those in the agricultural and natural resource sectors. The benefits of pollution-generating activities are usually far removed in both space and time from the costs. To make equitable decisions, therefore, one must consider both space and time factors. If wastes are dumped upstream, who will suffer downstream? If fungicides containing mercury are used now, to what extent, when, and where will the mercury appear in ocean fish? If polluting factories are located in remote areas to "isolate" the pollutants, where will those pollutants be ten or twenty years from now?

It may be that technological developments will allow the expansion of industry with decreasing pollution, but only at a high cost. The US Council on Environmental Quality has called for an expenditure of $105 billion between now and 1975 (42 percent of which is to be paid by industry) for just a partial cleanup of American air, water, and solid-waste pollution.[27] Any country can postpone the payment of such costs to increase the present growth rate of its capital plant, but only at the expense of future environmental degradation, which may be reversible only at very high cost.

A FINITE WORLD

We have mentioned many difficult trade-offs in this chapter in the production of food, in the consumption of resources, and in the generation and clean-up of pollution. By now it should be clear that all of these trade-offs arise from one simple fact—the earth is finite. The closer any human activity comes to the limit of the earth's ability to support that activity, the more apparent and unresolvable the trade-offs become. When there is plenty of unused arable land, there can be more people and also more food per person. When all the land is already used, the trade-off between more people or more food per person becomes a choice between absolutes.

In general, modern society has not learned to recognize and deal with these trade-offs. The apparent goal of the present world system is to produce more people with more (food, material goods, clean air and water) for each person. In this chapter we have noted that if society continues to strive for that goal, it will eventually reach one of many earthly limitations. As we shall see in the next chapter, it is not possible to foretell exactly which limitation will occur first or what the consequences will be, because there are many conceivable, unpredictable human responses to such a situation. It is possible, however, to investigate what conditions and what changes in the world system might lead society to collision with or accommodation to the limits to growth in a finite world.

CHAPTER III

GROWTH IN THE WORLD SYSTEM

In the circumference of a circle the beginning and end are common.

HERACLITUS, 500 B.C.

We have discussed food, nonrenewable resources, and pollution absorption as separate factors necessary for the growth and maintenance of population and industry. We have looked at the rate of growth in the demand for each of these factors and at the possible upper limits to the supply. By making simple extrapolations of the demand growth curves, we have attempted to estimate, roughly, how much longer growth of each of these factors might continue at its present rate of increase. Our conclusion from these extrapolations is one that many perceptive people have already realized—that the short doubling times of many of man's activities, combined with the immense quantities being doubled, will bring us close to the limits to growth of those activities surprisingly soon.

Extrapolation of present trends is a time-honored way of looking into the future, especially the very near future, and especially if the quantity being considered is not much influenced by other trends that are occurring elsewhere in the system. Of course, none of the five factors we are examining here is independent. Each interacts constantly with all the others. We have already mentioned some of these interactions. Population cannot grow without food, food production is increased by growth of capital, more capital requires more resources, discarded resources become pollution, pollution interferes with the growth of both population and food.

Furthermore, over long time periods each of these factors also feeds back to influence itself. The rate at which food production increases in the 1970's, for example, will have some effect on the size of the population in the 1980's, which will in turn determine the rate at which food production must increase for many years thereafter. Similarly, the rate of resource consumption in the next few years will influence both the size of the capital base that must be maintained and the amount of resources left in the earth. Existing capital and available resources will then interact to determine future resource supply and demand.

The five basic quantities, or levels—population, capital, food, nonrenewable resources, and pollution—are joined by still other interrelationships and feedback loops that we have not yet discussed. Clearly it is not possible to assess the long-term future of any of these levels without taking all the others into account. Yet even this relatively simple system has such a complicated structure that one cannot intuitively understand how it will behave in the future, or how a change in one variable might ultimately affect each of the others. To achieve such understanding, we must extend our intuitive capabilities so that we can follow the complex, interrelated behavior of many variables simultaneously.

In this chapter we describe the formal world model that we have used as a first step toward comprehending this complex world system. The model is simply an attempt to bring together the large body of knowledge that already exists about cause-and-effect relationships among the five levels listed above and to express that knowledge in terms of interlocking feedback loops. Since the world model is so important in understanding the causes of and limits to growth in the world system, we shall explain the model-building process in some detail.

In constructing the model, we followed four main steps:

1. We first listed the important causal relationships among the five levels and traced the feedback loop structure. To do so we consulted literature and professionals in many fields of study dealing with the areas of concern—demography, economics, agronomy, nutrition, geology, and ecology, for example. Our goal in this first step was to find the most basic structure that would reflect the major interactions between the five levels. We reasoned that elaborations on this basic structure, reflecting more detailed knowledge, could be added after the simple system was understood.
2. We then quantified each relationship as accurately as possible, using global data where they were available and characteristic local data where global measurements had not been made.
3. With the computer, we calculated the simultaneous operation of all these relationships over time. We then tested the effect of numerical changes in the basic assumptions to find the most critical determinants of the system's behavior.
4. Finally, we tested the effect on our global system of the

various policies that are currently being proposed to enhance or change the behavior of the system.

These steps were not necessarily followed serially, because often new information coming from a later step would lead us back to alter the basic feedback loop structure. There is not one inflexible world model; there is instead an evolving model that is continuously criticized and updated as our own understanding increases.

A summary of the present model, its purpose and limitations, the most important feedback loops it contains, and our general procedure for quantifying causal relationships follows.

THE PURPOSE OF THE WORLD MODEL

In this first simple world model, we are interested only in the broad behavior modes of the population-capital system. By *behavior modes* we mean the tendencies of the variables in the system (population or pollution, for example) to change as time progresses. A variable may increase, decrease, remain constant, oscillate, or combine several of these characteristic modes. For example, a population growing in a limited environment can approach the ultimate carrying capacity of that environment in several possible ways. It can adjust smoothly to an equilibrium below the environmental limit by means of a gradual decrease in growth rate, as shown below. It can over-

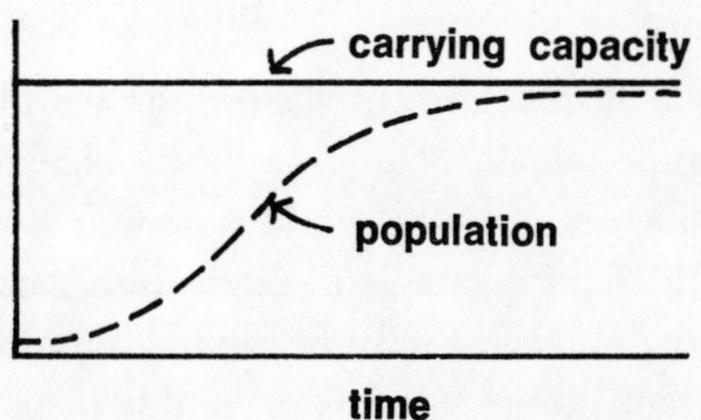

shoot the limit and then die back again in either a smooth or an oscillatory way, also as shown below. Or it can overshoot

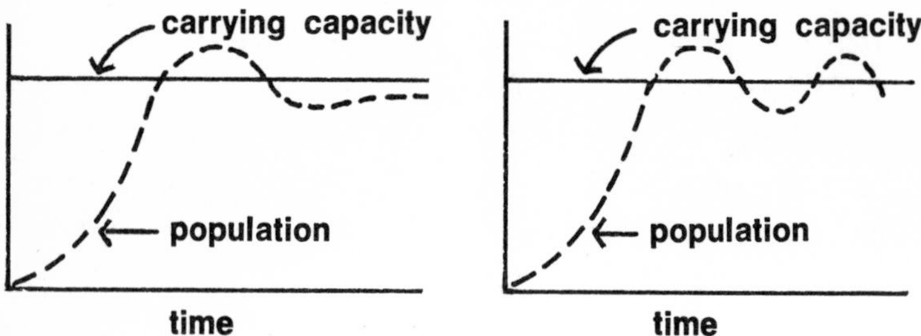

the limit and in the process decrease the ultimate carrying capacity by consuming some necessary nonrenewable resource, as diagramed below. This behavior has been noted in many natural systems. For instance, deer or goats, when natural enemies are absent, often overgraze their range and cause erosion or destruction of the vegetation.[28]

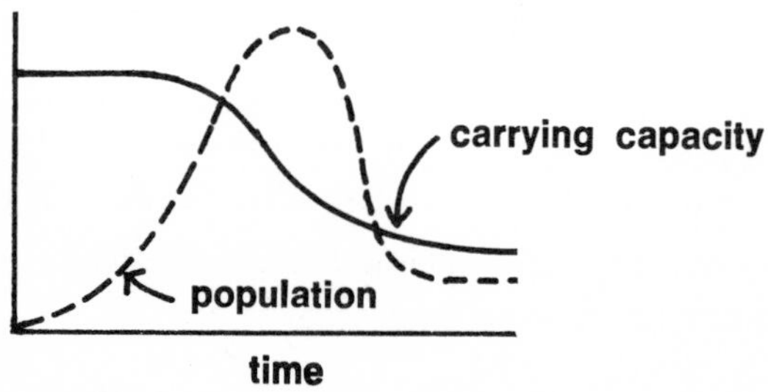

A major purpose in constructing the world model has been to determine which, if any, of these behavior modes will be most characteristic of the world system as it reaches the limits to growth. This process of determining behavior modes is "prediction" only in the most limited sense of the word. The output graphs reproduced later in this book show values for world population, capital, and other variables on a time scale that begins in the year 1900 and continues until 2100. These graphs are *not* exact predictions of the values of the variables at any particular year in the future. They are indications of the system's behavioral tendencies only.

The difference between the various degrees of "prediction" might be best illustrated by a simple example. If you throw a ball straight up into the air, you can predict with certainty what its general behavior will be. It will rise with decreasing velocity, then reverse direction and fall down with increasing velocity until it hits the ground. You know that it will not continue rising forever, nor begin to orbit the earth, nor loop three times before landing. It is this sort of elemental understanding of behavior modes that we are seeking with the present world model. If one wanted to predict exactly how high a thrown ball would rise or exactly where and when it would hit the ground, it would be necessary to make a detailed calculation based on precise information about the ball, the altitude, the wind, and the force of the initial throw. Similarly, if we wanted to predict the size of the earth's population in 1993 within a few percent, we would need a very much more complicated model than the one described here. We would also need information about the world system more precise and comprehensive than is currently available.

Because we are interested at this point only in broad behavior modes, this first world model need not be extremely detailed. We thus consider only one general population, a population that statistically reflects the average characteristics of the global population. We include only one class of pollutants—the long-lived, globally distributed family of pollutants, such as lead, mercury, asbestos, and stable pesticides and radioisotopes—

whose dynamic behavior in the ecosystem we are beginning to understand. We plot one generalized resource that represents the combined reserves of all nonrenewable resources, although we know that each separate resource will follow the general dynamic pattern at its own specific level and rate.

This high level of aggregation is necessary at this point to keep the model understandable. At the same time it limits the information we can expect to gain from the model. Questions of detail cannot be answered because the model simply does not yet contain much detail. National boundaries are not recognized. Distribution inequalities of food, resources, and capital are included implicitly in the data but they are not calculated explicitly nor graphed in the output. World trade balances, migration patterns, climatic determinants, and political processes are not specifically treated. Other models can, and we hope will, be built to clarify the behavior of these important subsystems.*

Can anything be learned from such a highly aggregated model? Can its output be considered meaningful? In terms of exact predictions, the output is not meaningful. We cannot forecast the precise population of the United States nor the GNP of Brazil nor even the total world food production for the year 2015. The data we have to work with are certainly not sufficient for such forecasts, even if it were our purpose to make them. On the other hand, it is vitally important to gain some understanding of the causes of growth in human society, the limits to growth, and the behavior of our socio-economic systems when the limits are reached. Man's knowledge of the

* We have built numerous submodels ourselves in the course of this study to investigate the detailed dynamics underlying each sector of the world model. A list of those studies is included in the appendix.

Figure 23 POPULATION GROWTH AND CAPITAL GROWTH FEEDBACK LOOPS

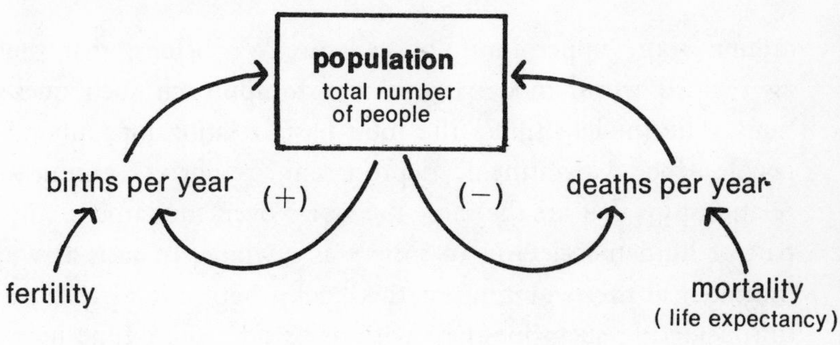

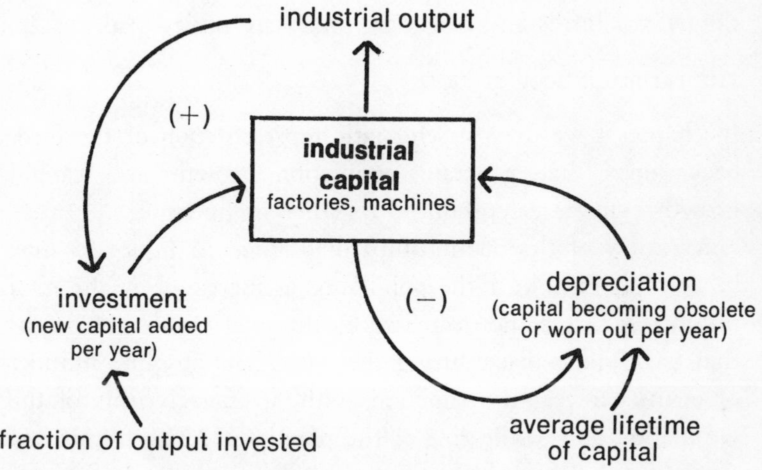

The central feedback loops of the world model govern the growth of population and of industrial capital. The two positive feedback loops involving births and investment generate the exponential growth behavior of population and capital. The two negative feedback loops involving deaths and depreciation tend to regulate this exponential growth. The relative strengths of the various loops depend on many other factors in the world system.

behavior modes of these systems is very incomplete. It is currently not known, for example, whether the human population will continue growing, or gradually level off, or oscillate around some upper limit, or collapse. We believe that the aggregated world model is one way to approach such questions. The model utilizes the most basic relationships among people, food, investment, depreciation, resources, output—relationships that are the same the world over, the same in any part of human society or in society as a whole. In fact, as we indicated at the beginning of this book, there are advantages to considering such questions with as broad a space-time horizon as possible. Questions of detail, of individual nations, and of short-term pressures can be asked much more sensibly when the overall limits and behavior modes are understood.

THE FEEDBACK LOOP STRUCTURE

In chapter I we drew a schematic representation of the feedback loops that generate population growth and capital growth. They are reproduced together in figure 23.

A review of the relationships diagramed in figure 23 may be helpful. Each year the population is increased by the total number of births and decreased by the total number of deaths that have taken place during that year. The absolute number of births per year is a function of the average fertility of the population and of the size of the population. The number of deaths is related to the average mortality and the total population size. As long as births exceed deaths, the population grows. Similarly, a given amount of industrial capital, operating at constant efficiency, will be able to produce a certain amount of output each year. Some of that output will be more factories, machines, etc., which are investments to increase the stock of capital goods. At the same time some capital equipment will depreciate or be discarded each year. To keep industrial capital growing, the investment rate must exceed the

Figure 24 FEEDBACK LOOPS OF POPULATION, CAPITAL, AGRICULTURE, AND POLLUTION

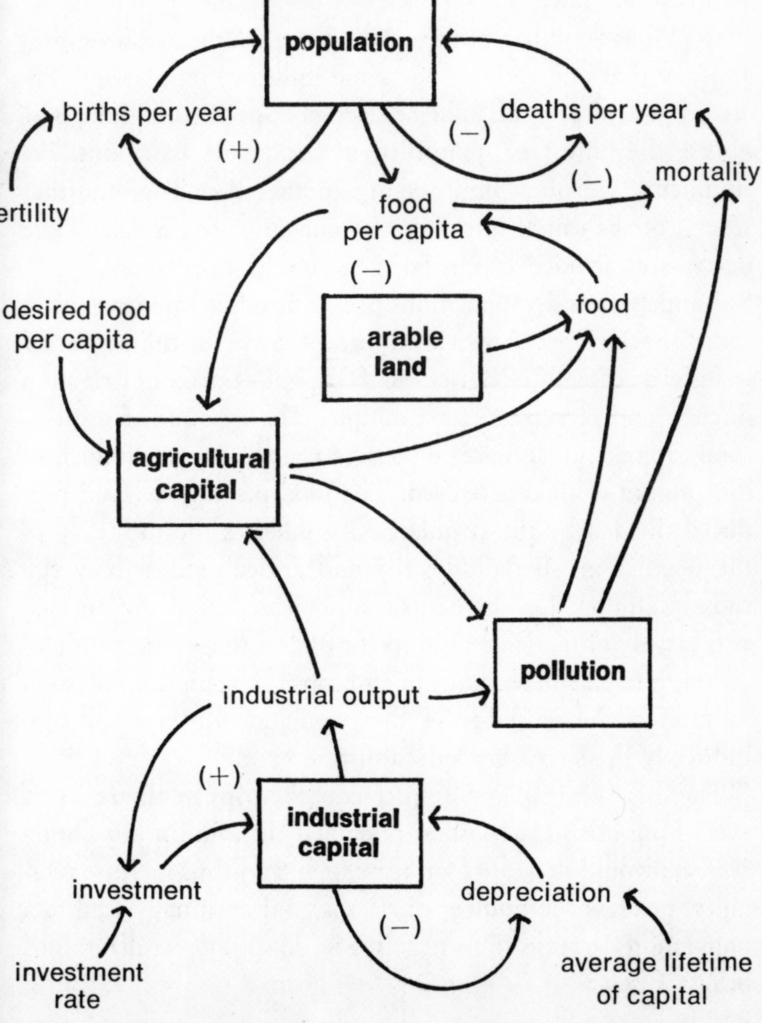

Some of the interconnections between population and industrial capital operate through agricultural capital, cultivated land, and pollution. Each arrow indicates a causal relationship, which may be immediate or delayed, large or small, positive or negative, depending on the assumptions included in each model run.

depreciation rate.

In all our flow diagrams, such as figure 23, the arrows simply indicate that one variable has some influence on another. The *nature* and *degree* of influence are not specified, although of course they must be quantified in the model equations. For simplicity, we often omit noting in the flow diagrams that several of the causal interactions occur only after a delay. The delays are included explicitly in the model calculations.

Population and capital influence each other in many ways, some of which are shown in figure 24. Some of the output of industrial capital is agricultural capital—tractors, irrigation ditches, and fertilizers, for example. The amount of agricultural capital and land area under cultivation strongly influences the amount of food produced. The food per capita (food produced divided by the population) influences the mortality of the population. Both industrial and agricultural activity can cause pollution. (In the case of agriculture, the pollution consists largely of pesticide residues, fertilizers that cause eutrophication, and salt deposits from improper irrigation.) Pollution may affect the mortality of the population directly and also indirectly by decreasing agricultural output.[29]

There are several important feedback loops in figure 24. If everything else in the system remained the same, a population *increase* would decrease food per capita, and thus increase mortality, increase the number of deaths, and eventually lead to a population decrease. This negative feedback loop is diagramed below.

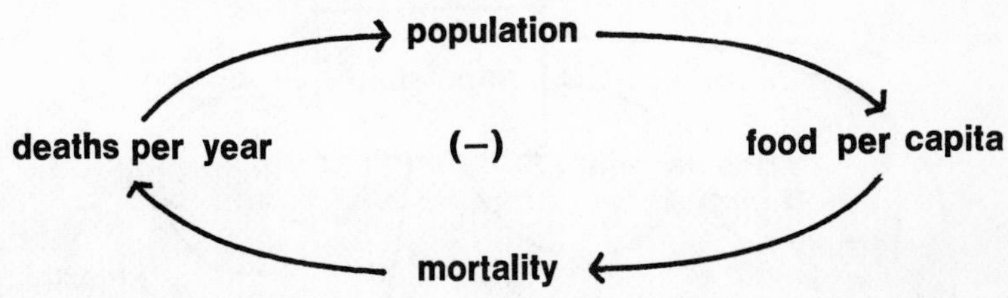

Another negative feedback loop (shown below) tends to counterbalance the one shown above. If the food per capita *decreases* to a value lower than that desired by the population, there will be a tendency to increase agricultural capital, so that future food production and food per capita can *increase*.

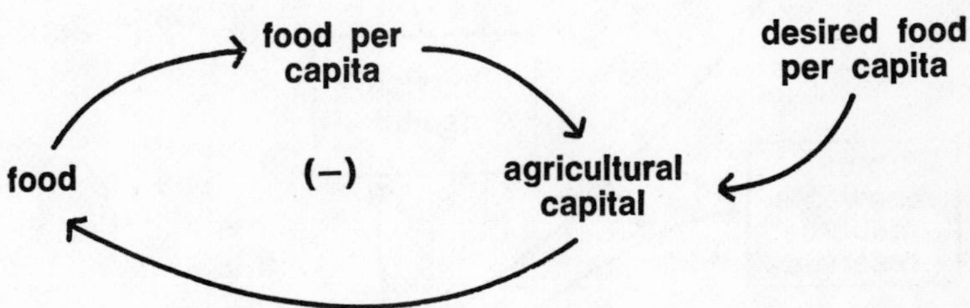

Other important relationships in the world model are illustrated in figure 25. These relationships deal with population, industrial capital, service capital, and resources.

Industrial output includes goods that are allocated to service capital—houses, schools, hospitals, banks, and the equipment they contain. The output from this service capital divided by the population gives the average value of services per capita. Services per capita influence the level of health services and thus the mortality of the population. Services also include education and research into birth control methods as well as distribution of birth control information and devices. Services per capita are thus related to fertility.

Figure 25 FEEDBACK LOOPS OF POPULATION, CAPITAL, SERVICES, AND RESOURCES

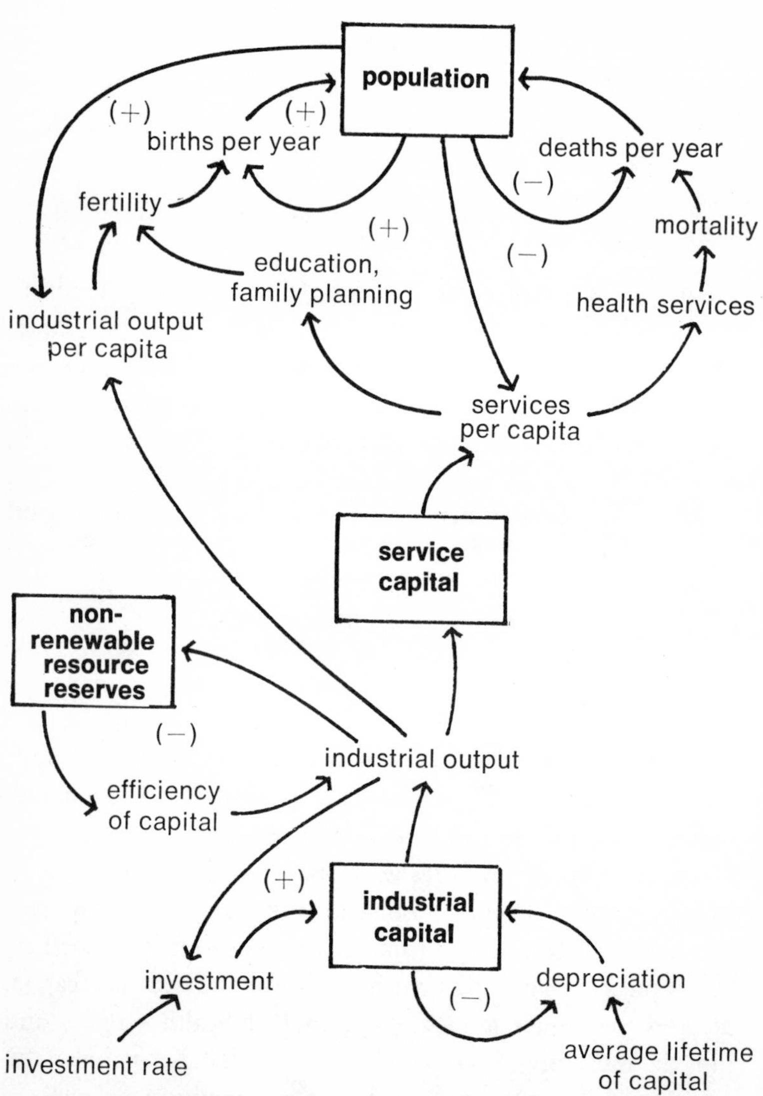

Population and industrial capital are also influenced by the levels of service capital (such as health and education services) and of nonrenewable resource reserves.

A changing industrial output per capita also has an observable effect (though typically after a long delay) on many social factors that influence fertility.

Each unit of industrial output consumes some nonrenewable resource reserves. As the reserves gradually diminish, more capital is necessary to extract the same amount of resource from the earth, and thus the efficiency of capital decreases (that is, more capital is required to produce a given amount of finished goods).

The important feedback loops in figure 25 are shown below.

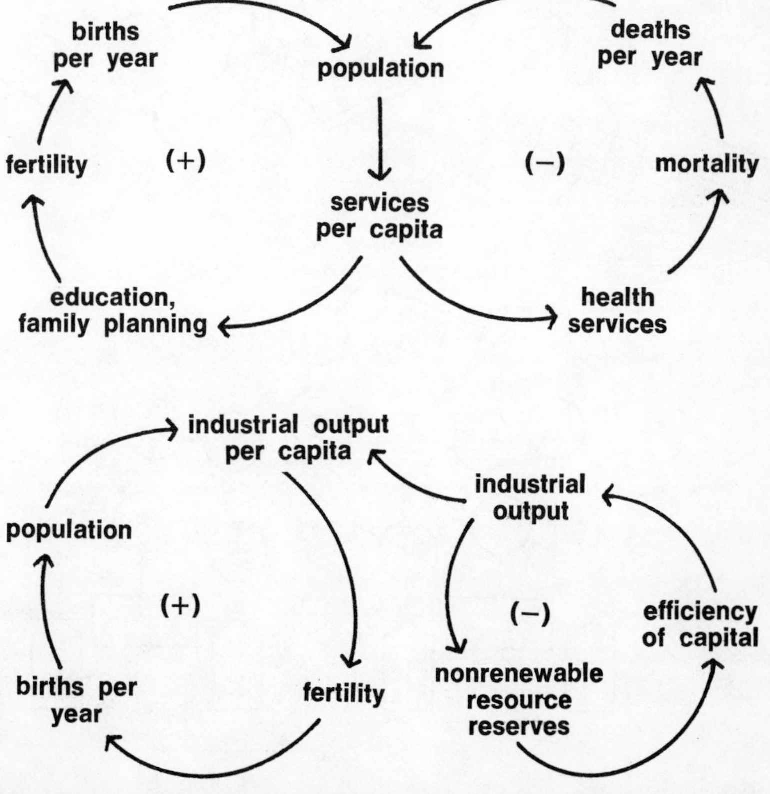

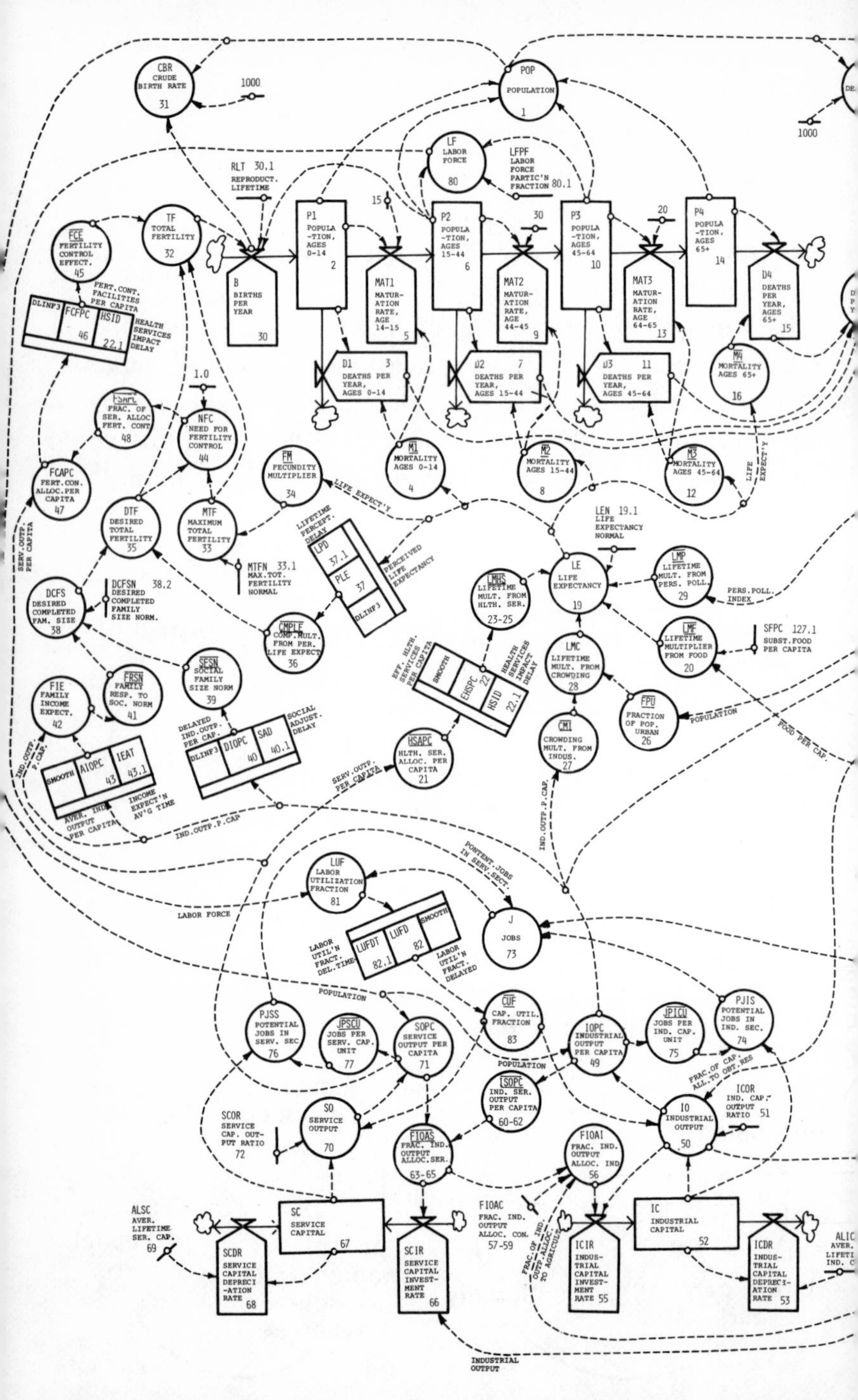

CBR CRUDE BIRTH RATE 31
1000
POP POPULATION 1
1000
LF LABOR FORCE 80
LFPF LABOR FORCE PARTIC'N FRACTION 80.1
RLT 30.1 REPRODUCT. LIFETIME
TF TOTAL FERTILITY 32
FCE FERTILITY CONTROL EFFECT. 45
FERT.CONT. FACILITIES PER CAPITA
DLINF3 FCFPC 46 HSID 22.1
HEALTH SERVICES IMPACT DELAY
B BIRTHS PER YEAR 30
P1 POPULA -TION, AGES 0-14 2
15
MAT1 MATUR-ATION RATE, AGE 14-15 5
P2 POPULA -TION, AGES 15-44 6
30
MAT2 MATUR-ATION RATE, AGE 44-45 9
P3 POPULA -TION, AGES 45-64 10
20
MAT3 MATUR-ATION RATE, AGE 64-65 13
P4 POPULA -TION, AGES 65+ 14
D4 DEATHS PER YEAR, AGES 65+ 15
D1 3 DEATHS PER YEAR, AGES 0-14
D2 7 DEATHS PER YEAR, AGES 15-44
D3 11 DEATHS PER YEAR, AGES 45-64
M4 MORTALITY AGES 65+ 16
1.0
FSAFC FRAC. OF SER. ALLOC FERT. CONT 48
NFC NEED FOR FERTILITY CONTROL 44
M1 MORTALITY AGES 0-14 4
M2 MORTALITY AGES 15-44 8
M3 MORTALITY AGES 45-64 12
LIFE EXPECT'Y
FCAPC FERT.CON. ALLOC.PER CAPITA 47
FM FECUNDITY MULTIPLIER 34
LIFE EXPECT'Y
DTF DESIRED TOTAL FERTILITY 35
MTF MAXIMUM TOTAL FERTILITY 33
LIFETIME PERCEPT. DELAY
LPD 37.1 PLE 37 DLINF3
PERCEIVED LIFE EXPECTANCY
LEN 19.1 LIFE EXPECTANCY NORMAL
SERV.OUTP. PER CAPITA
MTFN 33.1 MAX.TOT. FERTILITY NORMAL
DCFS DESIRED COMPLETED FAM. SIZE 38
DCFSN 38.2 DESIRED COMPLETED FAMILY SIZE NORM.
CMPLE COMP.MULT. FROM PER. LIFE EXPECT 36
LMHS LIFETIME MULT. FROM HLTH. SER. 23-25
LE LIFE EXPECTANCY 19
LMP LIFETIME MULT. FROM PERS. POLL. 29
PERS.POLL. INDEX
EFF. HLTH. SERVICES PER CAPITA
SMOOTH EHSPC 22 HSID 22.1
HEALTH SERVICES IMPACT DELAY
LMC LIFETIME MULT. FROM CROWDING 28
LMF LIFETIME MULTIPLIER FROM FOOD 20
SFPC 127.1 SUBST.FOOD PER CAPITA
FIE FAMILY INCOME EXPECT. 42
FRSN FAMILY RESP. TO SOC. NORM 41
SFSN SOCIAL FAMILY SIZE NORM 39
DELAYED IND.OUTP. PER CAP.
DLINF3 DIOPC 40 SAD 40.1
SOCIAL ADJUST. DELAY
CMI CROWDING MULT. FROM INDUS. 27
FPU FRACTION OF POP. URBAN 26
POPULATION
FOOD PER CAP.
IND.OUTP. P.CAP.
SMOOTH AIOPC 43 IEAT 43.1
AVER. IND. OUTPUT PER CAPITA
INCOME EXPECT'N AV'G TIME
SERV.OUTP. PER CAPITA
HSAPC HLTH. SER. ALLOC. PER CAPITA 21
IND.OUTP.P.CAP.
IND.OUTP.P.CAP.
POTENT.JOBS IN SERV.SECT.
LUF LABOR UTILIZATION FRACTION 81
LABOR FORCE
LUFDT 82.1 LUFD 82 SMOOTH
LABOR UTIL'N FRACT. DEL.TIME
LABOR UTIL'N FRACT. DELAYED
J JOBS 73
POPULATION
CUF CAP. UTIL. FRACTION 83
PJSS POTENTIAL JOBS IN SERV. SEC 76
JPSCU JOBS PER SERV. CAP. UNIT 77
SOPC SERVICE OUTPUT PER CAPITA 71
IOPC INDUSTRIAL OUTPUT PER CAPITA 49
JPICU JOBS PER IND. CAP. UNIT 75
PJIS POTENTIAL JOBS IN IND. SEC. 74
POPULATION
ISOPC IND. SER. OUTPUT PER CAPITA 60-62
FRAC.OF CAP. ALL.TO OBT.RES
ICOR IND. CAP. OUTPUT RATIO 51
SCOR SERVICE CAP. OUT-PUT RATIO 72
SO SERVICE OUTPUT 70
FIOAS FRAC. IND. OUTPUT ALLOC.SER. 63-65
FIOAI FRAC. IND. OUTPUT ALLOC. IND 56
IO INDUSTRIAL OUTPUT 50
ALSC AVER. LIFETIME SER. CAP. 69
SC SERVICE CAPITAL 67
FIOAC FRAC. IND. OUTPUT ALLOC. CON. 57-59
FRAC.OF IND. OUTP.ALLOC. TO AGRICUL
IC INDUSTRIAL CAPITAL 52
SCDR SERVICE CAPITAL DEPRECI -ATION RATE 68
SCIR SERVICE CAPITAL INVEST-MENT RATE 66
ICIR INDUS-TRIAL CAPITAL INVEST-MENT RATE 55
ICDR INDUS-TRIAL CAPITAL DEPRECI-ATION RATE 53
INDUSTRIAL OUTPUT

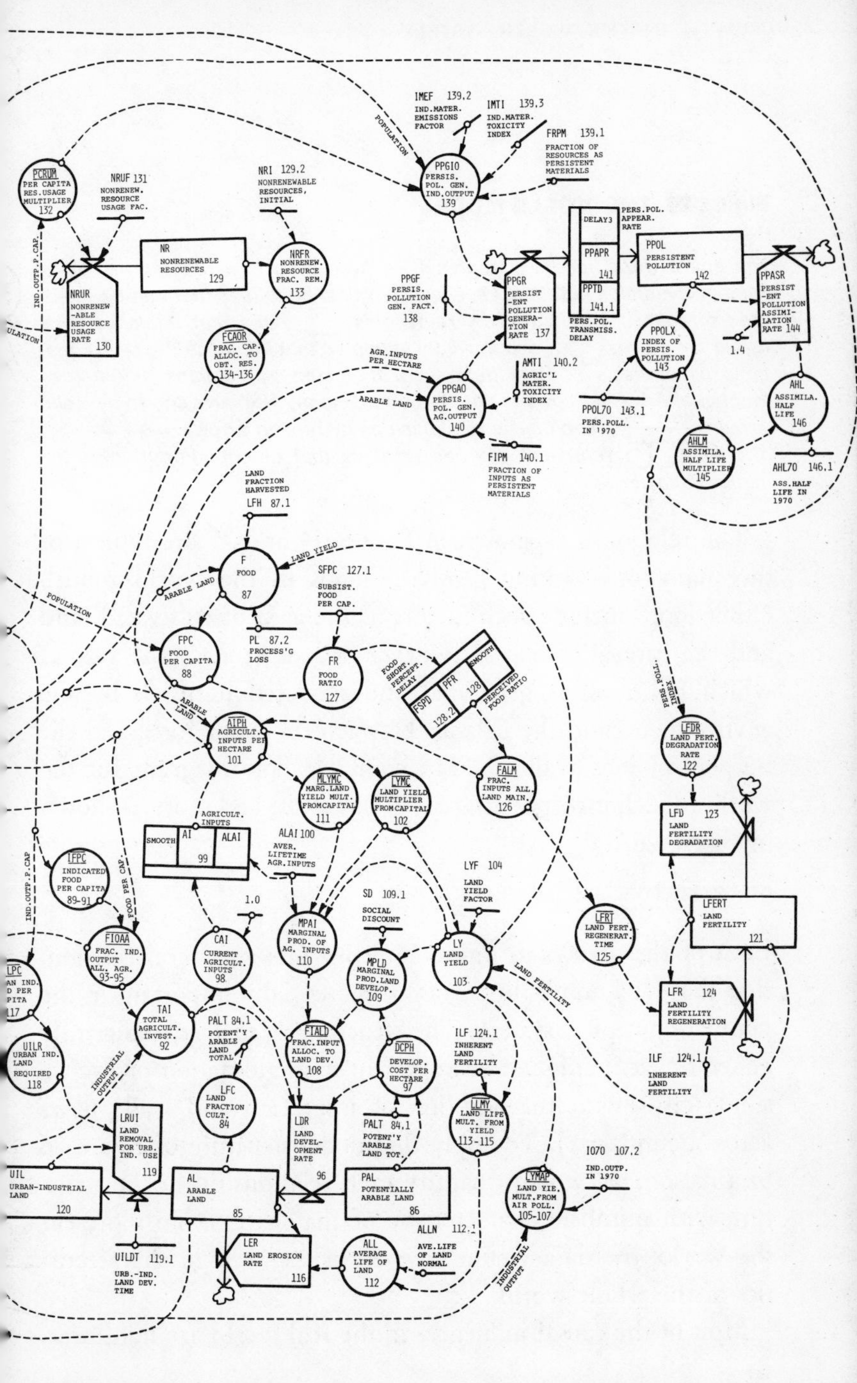

IMEF 139.2 IND.MATER. EMISSIONS FACTOR
IMTI 139.3 IND.MATER. TOXICITY INDEX
FRPM 139.1 FRACTION OF RESOURCES AS PERSISTENT MATERIALS
POPULATION
PPGIO PERSIS. POL. GEN. IND.OUTPUT 139
PCRUM PER CAPITA RES.USAGE MULTIPLIER 132
NRUF 131 NONRENEW. RESOURCE USAGE FAC.
NRI 129.2 NONRENEWABLE RESOURCES, INITIAL
NR NONRENEWABLE RESOURCES 129
NRFR NONRENEW. RESOURCE FRAC. REM. 133
NRUR NONRENEW -ABLE RESOURCE USAGE RATE 130
IND.OUTP.P.CAP.
FCAOR FRAC. CAP. ALLOC. TO OBT. RES. 134-136
DELAY3 PPAPR 141 PPTD 141.1
PERS.POL. APPEAR. RATE
PERS.POL. TRANSMISS. DELAY
PPOL PERSISTENT POLLUTION 142
PPASR PERSIST -ENT POLLUTION ASSIMI- LATION RATE 144
PPGF PERSIS. POLLUTION GEN. FACT. 138
PPGR PERSIST -ENT POLLUTION GENERA- TION RATE 137
PPOLX INDEX OF PERSIS. POLLUTION 143
1.4
AGR.INPUTS PER HECTARE
ARABLE LAND
PPGAO PERSIS. POL. GEN. AG.OUTPUT 140
AMTI 140.2 AGRIC'L MATER. TOXICITY INDEX
PPOL70 143.1 PERS.POLL. IN 1970
AHL ASSIMILA. HALF LIFE 146
AHLM ASSIMILA. HALF LIFE MULTIPLIER 145
AHL70 146.1 ASS.HALF LIFE IN 1970
FIPM 140.1 FRACTION OF INPUTS AS PERSISTENT MATERIALS
LAND FRACTION HARVESTED LFH 87.1
LAND YIELD
F FOOD 87
SFPC 127.1 SUBSIST. FOOD PER CAP.
PL 87.2 PROCESS'G LOSS
FPC FOOD PER CAPITA 88
FR FOOD RATIO 127
FOOD SHORT. PERCEPT. DELAY
FSPD 128.2 PFR 128 SMOOTH
PERCEIVED FOOD RATIO
PERS.POLL. INDEX
AIPH AGRICULT. INPUTS PER HECTARE 101
LFDR LAND FERT. DEGRADATION RATE 122
MLYMC MARG.LAND YIELD MULT. FROMCAPITAL 111
LYMC LAND YIELD MULTIPLIER FROMCAPITAL 102
FALM FRAC. INPUTS ALL. LAND MAIN. 126
LFD 123 LAND FERTILITY DEGRADATION
AGRICULT. INPUTS
SMOOTH AI 99 ALAI
ALAI 100 AVER. LIFETIME AGR.INPUTS
LYF 104 LAND YIELD FACTOR
IFPC INDICATED FOOD PER CAPITA 89-91
FOOD PER CAP.
SD 109.1 SOCIAL DISCOUNT
1.0
LFERT LAND FERTILITY 121
MPAI MARGINAL PROD. OF AG. INPUTS 110
FIOAA FRAC. IND. OUTPUT ALL. AGR. 93-95
CAI CURRENT AGRICULT. INPUTS 98
LY LAND YIELD 103
MPLD MARGINAL PROD.LAND DEVELOP. 109
LFRT LAND FERT. REGENERAT. TIME 125
LAND FERTILITY
LPC ...AN IND. ...D PER ...PITA ...117
TAI TOTAL AGRICULT. INVEST. 92
PALT 84.1 POTENT'Y ARABLE LAND TOTAL
FIALD FRAC.INPUT ALLOC. TO LAND DEV. 108
DCPH DEVELOP. COST PER HECTARE 97
ILF 124.1 INHERENT LAND FERTILITY
LFR 124 LAND FERTILITY REGENERATION
UILR URBAN IND. LAND REQUIRED 118
INDUSTRIAL OUTPUT
LFC LAND FRACTION CULT. 84
LLMY LAND LIFE MULT. FROM YIELD 113-115
LRUI LAND REMOVAL FOR URB. IND. USE 119
LDR LAND DEVEL- OPMENT RATE 96
PALT 84.1 POTENT'Y ARABLE LAND TOT.
IO70 107.2 IND.OUTP. IN 1970
UIL URBAN-INDUSTRIAL LAND 120
AL ARABLE LAND 85
PAL POTENTIALLY ARABLE LAND 86
LYMAP LAND YIE. MULT.FROM AIR POLL. 105-107
LER LAND EROSION RATE 116
ALL AVERAGE LIFE OF LAND 112
ALLN 112.1 AVE.LIFE OF LAND NORMAL
UILDT 119.1 URB.-IND. LAND DEV. TIME

Figure 26 THE WORLD MODEL

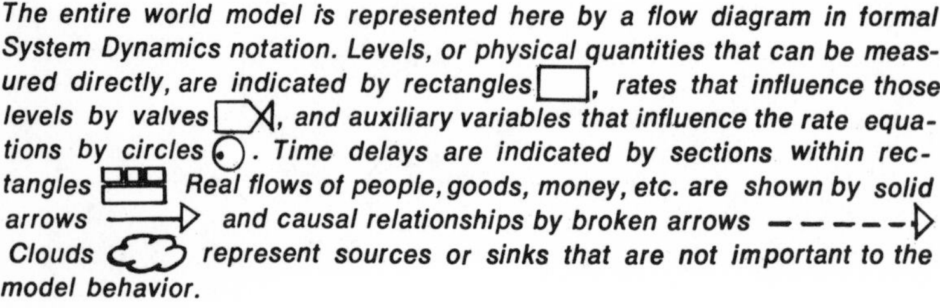

The entire world model is represented here by a flow diagram in formal System Dynamics notation. Levels, or physical quantities that can be measured directly, are indicated by rectangles, rates that influence those levels by valves, and auxiliary variables that influence the rate equations by circles. Time delays are indicated by sections within rectangles. Real flows of people, goods, money, etc. are shown by solid arrows and causal relationships by broken arrows. Clouds represent sources or sinks that are not important to the model behavior.

The relationships shown in figures 24 and 25 are typical of the many interlocking feedback loops in the world model. Other loops include such factors as the area of cultivated land and the rate at which it is developed or eroded, the rate at which pollution is generated and rendered harmless by the environment, and the balance between the labor force and the number of jobs available. The complete flow diagram for the world model, incorporating all these factors and more, is shown in figure 26.

QUANTITATIVE ASSUMPTIONS

Each of the arrows in figure 26 represents a general relationship that we know is important or potentially important in the population-capital system. The structure is, in fact, sufficiently general that it might also represent a single nation or even a single city (with the addition of migration and trade flows across boundaries). To apply the model structure of figure 26 to a nation, we would quantify each relationship in the structure with numbers characteristic of that nation. To represent the world, the data would have to reflect average characteristics of the whole world.

Most of the causal influences in the real world are nonlinear.

That is, a certain change in a causal variable (such as an increase of 10 percent in food per capita) may affect another variable (life expectancy, for example) differently, depending on the point within the possible range of the second variable at which the change takes place. For instance, if an increase in food per capita of 10 percent has been shown to increase life expectancy by 10 years, it may not follow that an increase of food per capita by 20 percent will increase life expectancy by 20 years. Figure 27 shows the nonlinearity of the relationship between food per capita and life expectancy. If there is little food, a small increase may bring about a large increase in life expectancy of a population. If there is already sufficient food, a further increase will have little or no effect. Nonlinear relationships of this sort have been incorporated directly into the world model.*

The current state of knowledge about causal relationships in the world ranges from complete ignorance to extreme accuracy. The relationships in the world model generally fall in the middle ground of certainty. We do know something about the direction and magnitude of the causal effects, but we rarely have fully accurate information about them. To illustrate how we operate on this intermediate ground of knowledge, we present here three examples of quantitative relationships from the world model. One is a relationship between economic variables that is relatively well understood; another involves socio-psychological variables that are well studied but difficult to quantify; and the third one relates biological variables that

* The data in figure 27 have not been corrected for variations in other factors, such as health care. Further information on statistical treatment of such a relationship and on its incorporation into the model equations is presented in the technical report.

Figure 27 NUTRITION AND LIFE EXPECTANCY

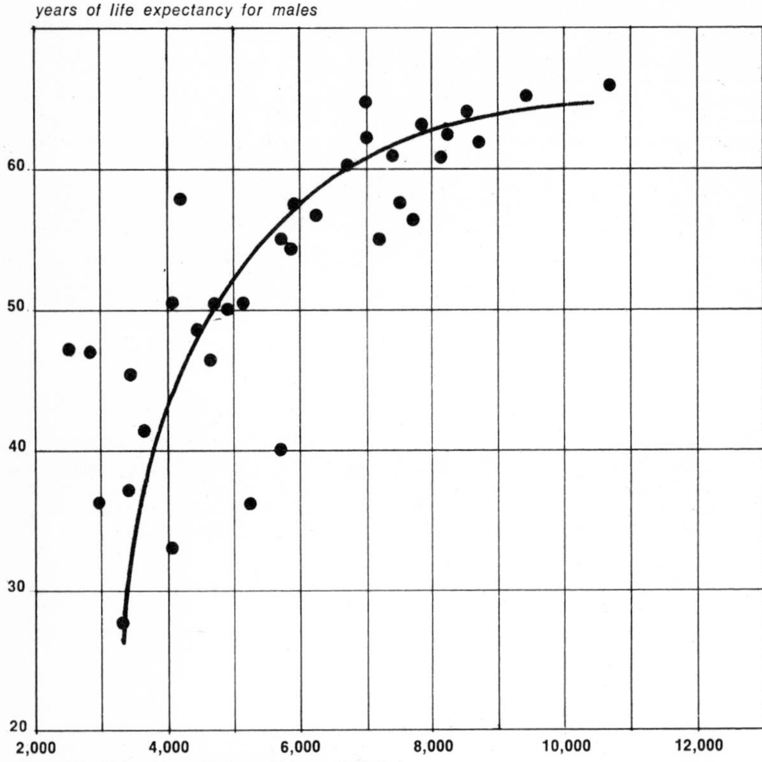

Life expectancy of a population is a nonlinear function of the nutrition that the population receives. In this graph nutritional level is given in vegetable calorie equivalents. Calories obtained from animal sources, such as meat or milk, are multiplied by a conversion factor (roughly 7, since about 7 calories of vegetable feed are required to produce 1 calorie of animal origin). Since food from animal sources is of greater value in sustaining human life, this measure takes into account both quantity and quality of food. Each point on the graph represents the average life expectancy and nutritional level of one nation in 1953.

SOURCE: M. Cépède, F. Houtart, and L. Grond, *Population and Food* (New York: Sheed and Ward, 1964).

are, as yet, almost totally unknown. Although these three examples by no means constitute a complete description of the world model, they illustrate the reasoning we have used to construct and quantify it.

Per capita resource use

As the world's population and capital plant grow, what will happen to the demand for nonrenewable resources? The amount of resources consumed each year can be found by multiplying the population times the per capita resource usage rate. Per capita resource usage rate is not constant, of course. As a population becomes more wealthy, it tends to consume more resources per person per year. The flow diagram expressing the relationship of population, per capita resource usage rate, and wealth (as measured by industrial output per capita) to the resource usage rate is shown below.

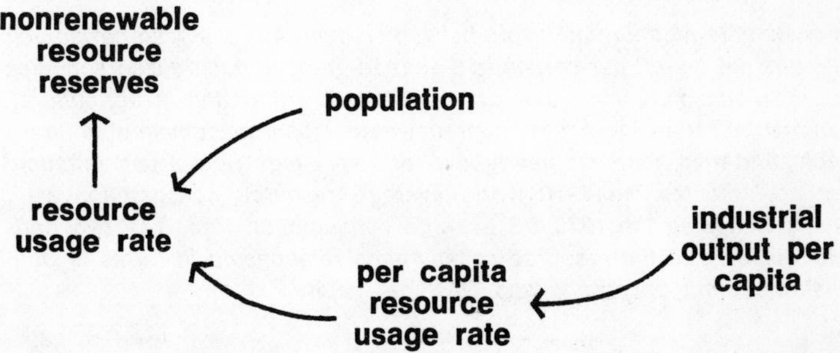

The relationship between wealth (industrial output per capita) and resource demand (per capita resource usage rate) is expressed by a nonlinear curve of the form shown in figure 28. In figure 28 resource use is defined in terms of the world average resource consumption per capita in 1970, which is set

Figure 28 INDUSTRIAL OUTPUT PER CAPITA AND RESOURCE USAGE

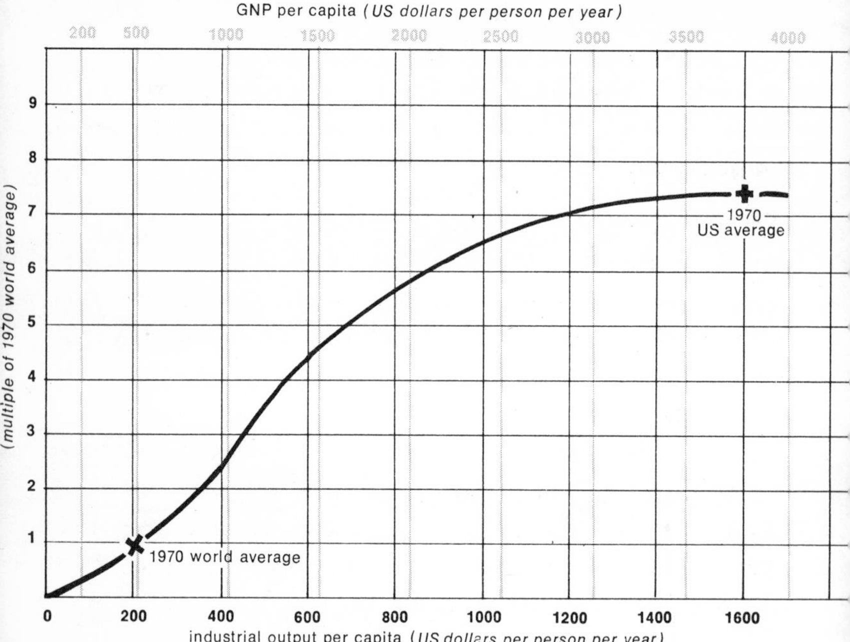

The postulated model relationship between resources consumed per person and industrial output per person is S-shaped. In nonindustrialized societies resource consumption is very low, since most production is agricultural. As industrialization increases, nonrenewable resource consumption rises steeply, and then becomes nearly level at a very high rate of consumption. Point × indicates the 1970 world average resource consumption rate; point + indicates the 1970 US average consumption rate. The two horizontal scales give the resource consumption relationship in terms of both industrial output per capita and GNP per capita.

equal to 1. Since world average industrial output per capita in 1970 was about $230,[30] we know that the curve goes through the point marked by an ×. In 1970 the United States had an average industrial output per capita of about $1,600, and the average citizen consumed approximately seven times the world average per capita resource usage.[31] The point on the curve that would represent the US level of consumption is marked by a +. We assume that, as the rest of the world develops economically, it will follow basically the US pattern of consumption—a sharp upward curve as output per capita grows, followed by a leveling off. Justification for that assumption can be found in the present pattern of world steel consumption (see figure 29). Although there is some variation in the steel consumption curve from the general curve of figure 28, the overall pattern is consistent, even given the differing economic and political structures represented by the various nations.

Additional evidence for the general shape of the resource consumption curve is shown by the history of US consumption of steel and copper plotted in figure 30. As the average individual income has grown, the resource usage in both cases has risen, at first steeply and then less steeply. The final plateau represents an average saturation level of material possessions. Further income increases are spent primarily on services, which are less resource consuming.

The S-shaped curve of resource usage shown in figure 28 is included in the world model only as a representation of apparent *present* policies. The curve can be altered at any time in the model simulation to test the effects of system changes (such as recycling of resources) that would either increase or decrease the amount of nonrenewable resources each person consumes. Actual model runs shown later in this book will illustrate the effects of such policies.

Desired birth rate

The number of births per year in any population equals the number of women of reproductive age times the average fertility (the average number of births per woman per year). There may be numerous factors influencing the fertility of a

Figure 29 WORLD STEEL CONSUMPTION AND GNP PER CAPITA

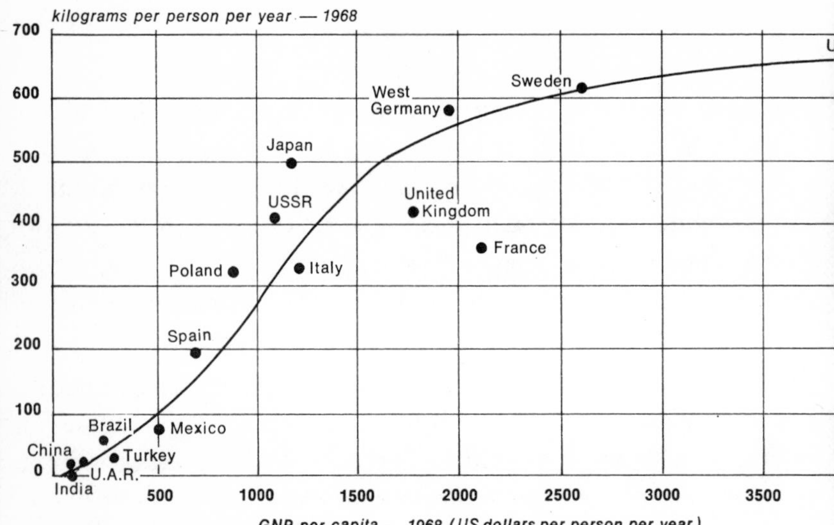

1968 steel consumption per person in various nations of the world follows the general S-shaped pattern shown in figure 28.

SOURCES: Steel consumption from UN Department of Economic and Social Affairs, *Statistical Yearbook 1969* (New York: United Nations, 1970). GNP per capita from *World Bank Atlas* (Washington, DC: International Bank for Reconstruction and Development, 1970).

population. In fact the study of fertility determinants is a major occupation of many of the world's demographers. In the world model we have identified three major components of fertility—maximum biological birth rate, birth control effectiveness, and desired birth rate. The relationship of these components to fertility is expressed in the diagram below.

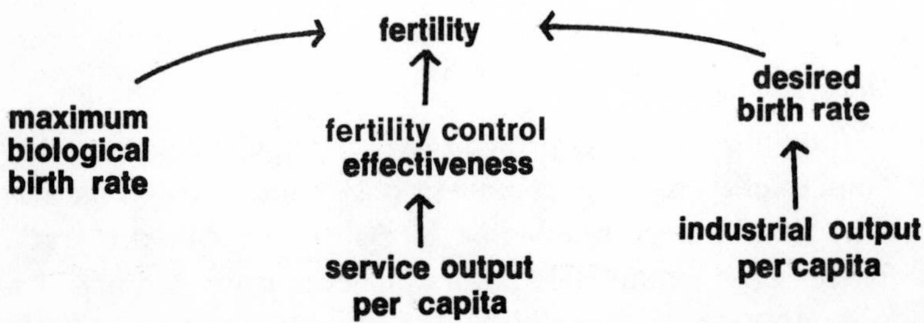

Figure 30 US COPPER AND STEEL CONSUMPTION AND GNP PER CAPITA

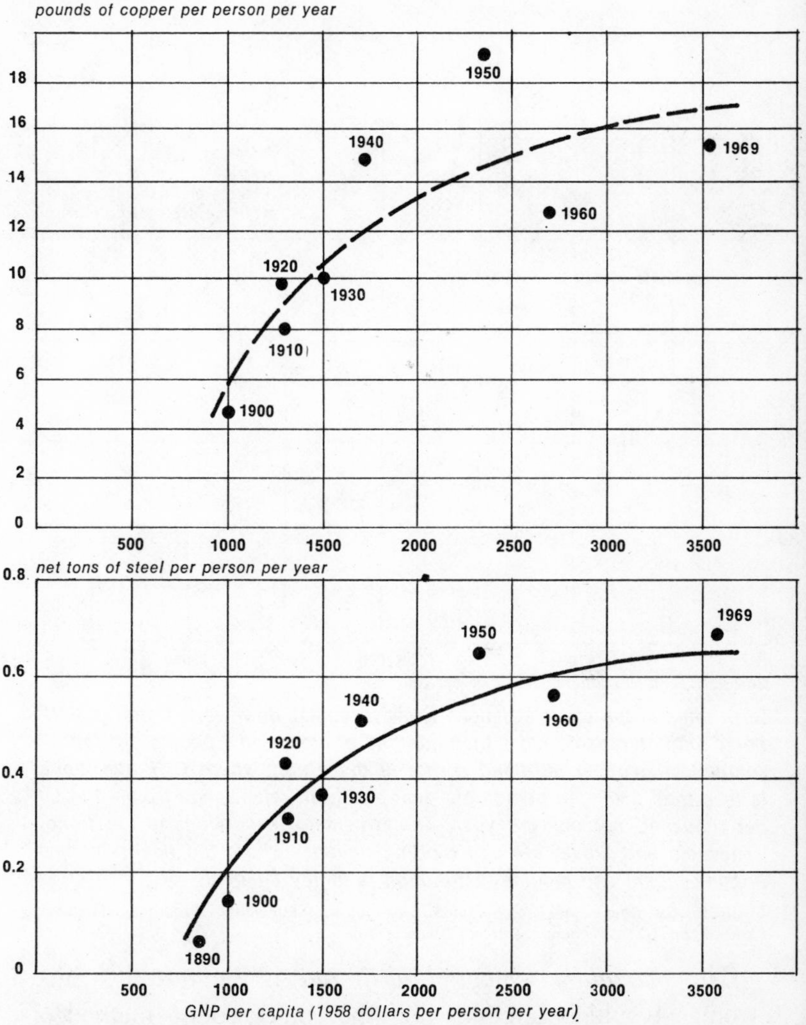

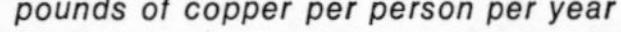

Per capita copper and steel consumption in the United States underwent a period of rapid increase as total productivity rose, followed by a period of much slower increase after consumption reached a relatively high rate.

SOURCES: Copper and steel consumption from *Metal Statistics* (Somerset, NJ: American Metal Market Company, 1970). Historical population and GNP from US Department of Commerce, *US Economic Growth* (Washington, DC: Government Printing Office, 1969).

Figure 31 BIRTH RATES AND GNP PER CAPITA

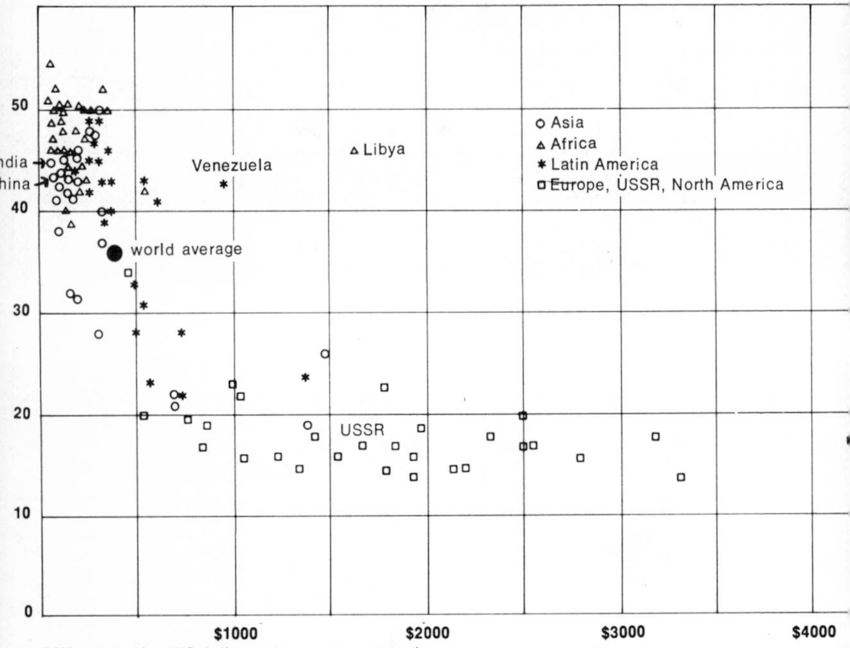

Birth rates in the world's nations show a regular downward trend as GNP per capita increases. More than one-half of the world's people are represented in the upper left-hand corner of the graph, where GNP per capita is less than $500 per person per year and birth rates range from 40 to 50 per thousand persons per year. The two major exceptions to the trend, Venezuela and Libya, are oil-exporting nations, where the rise in income is quite recent and income distribution is highly unequal.

SOURCE: US Agency for International Development, *Population Program Assistance* (Washington, DC: Government Printing Office, 1970).

The *maximum biological birth rate* is the rate at which women would bear children if they practiced no method of birth control throughout their entire reproductive lifetimes. This rate is biologically determined, depending mainly on the general health of the population. The *desired birth rate* is the rate that would result if the population practiced "perfect" birth control and had only planned and wanted children. *Birth control effectiveness* measures the extent to which the population is able to achieve the desired birth rate rather than the maximum biological one. Thus "birth control" is defined very broadly to include any method of controlling births actually practiced by a population, including contraception, abortion, and sexual abstinence. It should be emphasized that perfect birth control effectiveness does *not* imply low fertility. If desired birth rate is high, fertility will also be high.

These three factors influencing fertility are in turn influenced by other factors in the world system. Figure 31 suggests that industrialization might be one of the more important of these factors.

The relation between crude birth rates and GNP per capita of all the nations in the world follows a surprisingly regular pattern. In general, as GNP rises, the birth rate falls. This appears to be true, despite differences in religious, cultural, or political factors. Of course, we cannot conclude from this figure that a rising GNP per capita directly causes a lower birth rate. Apparently, however, a number of social and educational changes that ultimately lower the birth rate are associated with increasing industrialization. These social changes typically occur only after a rather long delay.

Where in the feedback loop structure does this inverse relationship between birth rate and per capita GNP operate? Most evidence would indicate that it does not operate through the maximum biological birth rate. If anything, rising industrialization implies better health, so that the number of births possible might increase as GNP increases. On the other hand, birth control effectiveness would also increase, and this effect certainly contributes to the decline in births shown in figure 31.

Figure 32 FAMILIES WANTING FOUR OR MORE CHILDREN AND GNP PER CAPITA

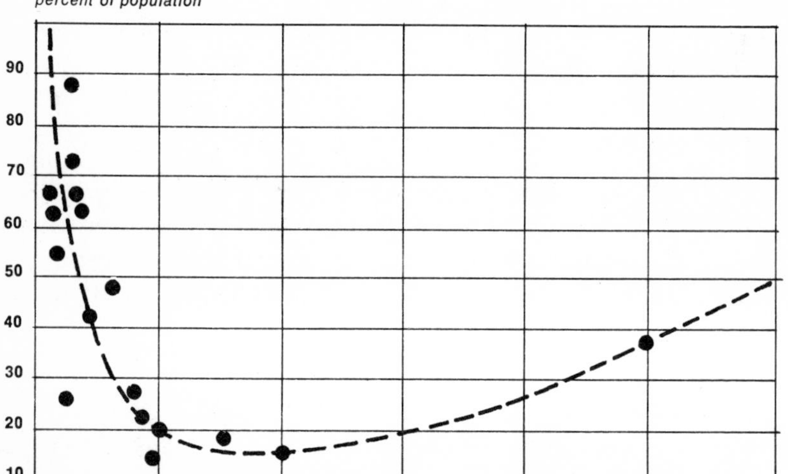

Respondents to family planning surveys in seventeen different countries indicated how many children they would like to have. The percentage of respondents desiring large families (four or more children) shows a relationship to average GNP per capita comparable to the trend shown in figure 31.

SOURCE: Bernard Berelson et al., *Family Planning and Population Programs* (Chicago: University of Chicago Press, 1965).

We suggest, however, that the major effect of rising GNP is on the *desired* birth rate. Evidence for this suggestion is shown in figure 32. The curve indicates the percentage of respondents to family planning surveys wanting more than four children as a function of GNP per capita. The general shape of the curve is similar to that of figure 31, except for the slight increase in desired family size at high incomes.

The economist J. J. Spengler has explained the general response of desired birth rate to income in terms of the economic and social changes that occur during the process of

Figure 33 DESIRED FAMILY SIZE

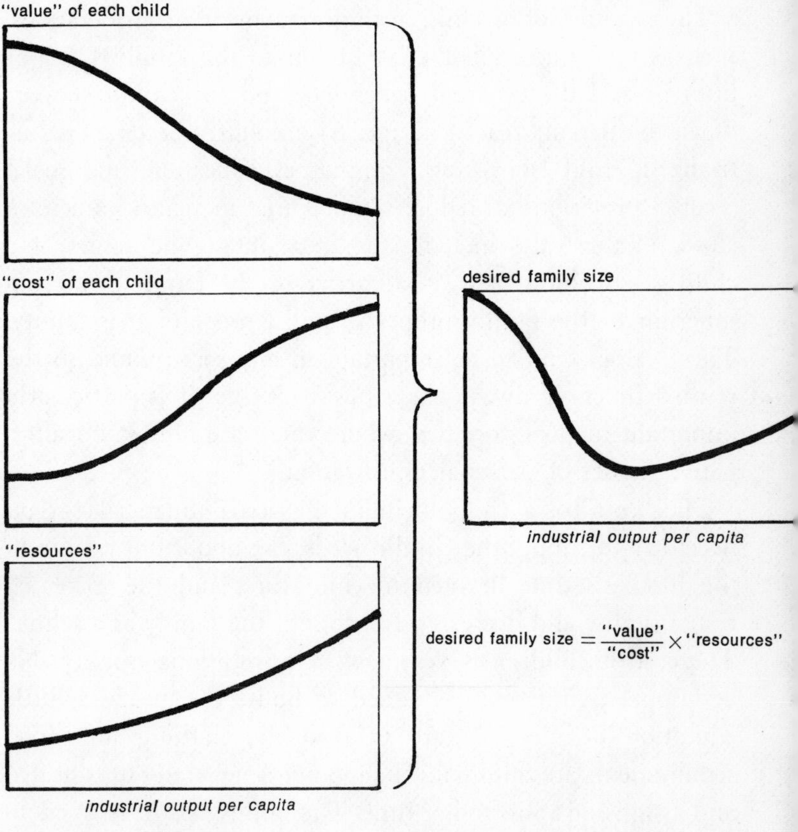

"value" of each child

"cost" of each child

"resources"

industrial output per capita

desired family size

industrial output per capita

$$\text{desired family size} = \frac{\text{"value"}}{\text{"cost"}} \times \text{"resources"}$$

Schematic representation of the economic determinants of family size follows a rough cost-benefit analysis. The resultant curve summarizes the balance between value and cost of children and resources available for child-raising, all as a function of increasing industrialization. This composite curve is similar to the curves in figures 31 and 32.

industrialization.[32] He believes that each family, consciously or unconsciously, weighs the value and cost of an additional child against the resources the family has available to devote to that child. This process results in a general attitude about family size that shifts as income increases, as shown in figure 33.

The "value" of a child includes monetary considerations, such as the child's labor contribution to the family farm or business and the eventual dependence on the child's support when the parents reach old age. As a country becomes industrialized, child labor laws, compulsory education, and social security provisions all reduce the potential monetary value of a child. "Value" also includes the more intangible values of a child as an object of love, a carrier of the family name, an inheritor of the family property, and a proof of masculinity. These values tend to be important in any society, and so the reward function always has a positive value. It is particularly important in poor societies, where there are almost no alternative modes of personal gratification.

The "cost" of a child includes the actual financial outlays necessary to supply the child's needs, the opportunity costs of the mother's time devoted to child care, and the increased responsibility and decreased freedom of the family as a whole. The cost of children is very low in a traditional society. No additional living space is added to house a new child, little education or medical care is available, clothing and food requirements are minimal. The mother is generally uneducated and assigns no value to her time. The family has little freedom to do anything that a child would hinder, and the extended family structure is there to provide child care if it should become necessary, for example, for a parent to leave home to find a job.

As family income increases, however, children are given more than the basic food and clothing requirements. They receive better housing and medical care, and education becomes both necessary and expensive. Travel, recreation, and alternative employment for the mother become possibilities that are not compatible with a large family. The extended family structure tends to disappear with industrialization, and substitute child care is costly.

The "resources" that a family has to devote to a child generally increase with income. At very high income, the value and cost curves become nearly invariant with further increases in income, and the resource curve becomes the dominant factor in the composite desired birth rate. Thus, in rich countries, such as the United States, desired family size becomes a direct function of income. It should be noted that "resources" is partially a psychological concept in that present actual income must be modified by an expectation of future income in planning family size.

We have summarized all these social factors by a feedback loop link between industrial output per capita and desired birth rate. The general shape of the relationship is shown on the right side of figure 33. We do not mean to imply by this link that rising income is the only determinant of desired family size, or even that it is a direct determinant. In fact we include a delay between industrial output per capita and desired family size to indicate that this relationship requires a social adjustment, which may take a generation or two to complete. Again, this relationship may be altered by future policies or social changes. As it stands it simply reflects the historical behavior of human society. Wherever economic development has taken place, birth rates have fallen. Where industrialization has not occurred, birth rates have remained high.

Pollution effect on lifetime

We have included in the world model the possibility that

pollution will influence the life expectancy of the world's population. We express this relationship by a "lifetime multiplier from pollution," a function that multiplies the life expectancy otherwise indicated (from the values of food and medical services) by the contribution to be expected from pollution. If pollution were severe enough to lower the life expectancy to 90 percent of its value in the absence of pollution, the multiplier would equal 0.9. The relationship of pollution to life expectancy is diagramed below.

There are only meager global data on the effect of pollution on life expectancy. Information is slowly becoming available about the toxicity to humans of specific pollutants, such as mercury and lead. Attempts to relate statistically a given concentration of pollutant to the mortality of a population have been made only in the field of air pollution.[33]

Although quantitative evidence is not yet available, there is little doubt that a relationship does indeed exist between pollution and human health. According to a recent Council on Environmental Quality report:

> Serious air pollution episodes have demonstrated how air pollution can severely impair health. Further research is spawning a growing body of evidence which indicates that even the long-term effects of exposure to low concentrations of pollutants can damage health and cause chronic disease and premature death, especially for the most vulnerable—the aged and those already suffering from respiratory diseases. Major illnesses linked to air pollution include emphysema, bronchitis, asthma, and lung cancer.[34]

What will be the effect on human lifetime as the present level of global pollution increases? We cannot answer this question accurately, but we do know that there will be *some* effect. We would be more in error to ignore the influence of pollution on life expectancy in the world model than to include it with our best guess of its magnitude. Our approach to a "best guess" is explained below and illustrated in figure 34.

If an increase in pollution by a factor of 100 times the present global level would have absolutely no effect on lifetime, the straight line A in figure 34 would be the correct representation of the relationship we seek. Life expectancy would be unrelated to pollution. Curve A is very unlikely, of course, since we know that many forms of pollution are damaging to the human body. Curve B or any similar curve that rises above curve A is even more unlikely since it indicates that additional pollution will increase average lifetime. We can expect that the relationship between pollution and lifetime is negative, although we do not know what the exact shape or slope of a curve expressing it will be. Any one of the curves labeled C, or any other negative curve, might represent the correct function.

Our procedure in a case like this is to make several different estimates of the probable effect of one variable on another and then to test each estimate in the model. If the model behavior is very sensitive to small changes in a curve, we know we must obtain more information before including it. If (as in this case) the behavior mode of the entire model is not substantially altered by changes in the curve, we make a conservative guess of its shape and include the corresponding values in our calculation. Curve C″ in figure 34 is the one we believe most accurately depicts the relationship between life expectancy

Figure 34 THE EFFECT OF POLLUTION ON LIFETIME

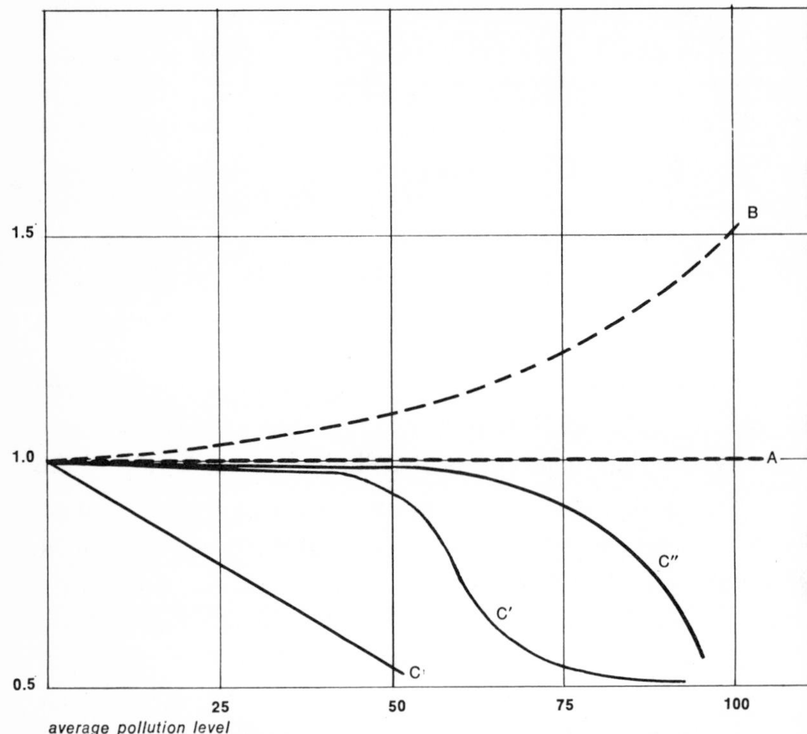

The relationship between level of pollution and average human lifetime might follow many different curves. Curve A indicates that pollution has no effect on lifetime (normal life expectancy is multiplied by 1.0). Curve B represents an enhancement of lifetime as pollution increases (normal life expectancy is multiplied by a number greater than 1.0). The curves C, C′, and C″ reflect differing assumptions about deleterious effects of pollution on lifetime. The relationship used in the world model is shaped like curve C″.

and pollution. This curve assumes that an increase in global pollution by a factor of 10 would have almost no effect on lifetime but an increase by a factor of 100 would have a great effect.

The usefulness of the world model

The relationships discussed above comprise only three of the hundred or so causal links that make up the world model. They have been chosen for presentation here as examples of the kind of information inputs we have used and the way in which we have used them. In many cases the information available is not complete. Nevertheless, we believe that the model based on this information is useful even at this preliminary stage for several reasons.

First, we hope that by posing each relationship as a hypothesis, and emphasizing its importance in the total world system, we may generate discussion and research that will eventually improve the data we have to work with. This emphasis is especially important in the areas in which different sectors of the model interact (such as pollution and human lifetime), where interdisciplinary research will be necessary.

Second, even in the absence of improved data, information now available is sufficient to generate valid basic behavior modes for the world system. This is true because the model's feedback loop structure is a much more important determinant of overall behavior than the exact numbers used to quantify the feedback loops. Even rather large changes in input data do not generally alter the *mode* of behavior, as we shall see in the following pages. Numerical changes may well affect the *period* of an oscillation or the *rate* of growth or the *time* of a collapse, but they will not affect the fact that the basic mode is oscillation or growth or collapse.* Since we intend to use the

---

* The importance of structure rather than numbers is a most difficult concept to present without extensive examples from the observation and modeling of dynamic systems. For further discussion of this point, see chapter 6 of J. W. Forrester's *Urban Dynamics* (Cambridge, Mass.: MIT Press, 1969).

world model only to answer questions about behavior modes, not to make exact predictions, we are primarily concerned with the correctness of the feedback loop structure and only secondarily with the accuracy of the data. Of course when we do begin to seek more detailed, short-term knowledge, exact numbers will become much more important.

Third, if decision-makers at any level had access to precise predictions and scientifically correct analyses of alternate policies, we would certainly not bother to construct or publish a simulation model based on partial knowledge. Unfortunately, there is no perfect model available for use in evaluating today's important policy issues. At the moment, our only alternatives to a model like this, based on partial knowledge, are mental models, based on the mixture of incomplete information and intuition that currently lies behind most political decisions. A dynamic model deals with the same incomplete information available to an intuitive model, but it allows the organization of information from many different sources into a feedback loop structure that can be exactly analyzed. Once all the assumptions are together and written down, they can be exposed to criticism, and the system's response to alternative policies can be tested.

WORLD MODEL BEHAVIOR

Now we are at last in a position to consider seriously the questions we raised at the beginning of this chapter. As the world system grows toward its ultimate limits, what will be its most likely behavior mode? What relationships now existent will change as the exponential growth curves level off? What will the world be like when growth comes to an end?

There are, of course, many possible answers to these questions. We will examine several alternatives, each dependent on a different set of assumptions about how human society will respond to problems arising from the various limits to growth.

Let us begin by assuming that there will be in the future no great changes in human values nor in the functioning of the global population-capital system as it has operated for the last one hundred years. The results of this assumption are shown in figure 35. We shall refer to this computer output as the "standard run" and use it for comparison with the runs based on other assumptions that follow. The horizontal scale in figure 35 shows time in years from 1900 to 2100. With the computer we have plotted the progress over time of eight quantities:

- population (total number of persons)
- industrial output per capita (dollar equivalent per person per year)
- food per capita (kilogram-grain equivalent per person per year)
- pollution (multiple of 1970 level)
- nonrenewable resources (fraction of 1900 reserves remaining)
- B crude birth rate (births per 1000 persons per year)
- D crude death rate (deaths per 1000 persons per year)
- S services per capita (dollar equivalent per person per year)

Each of these variables is plotted on a different vertical scale. We have deliberately omitted the vertical scales and we have made the horizontal time scale somewhat vague because we want to emphasize the general behavior modes of these computer outputs, not the numerical values, which are only approxi-

Figure 35 WORLD MODEL STANDARD RUN

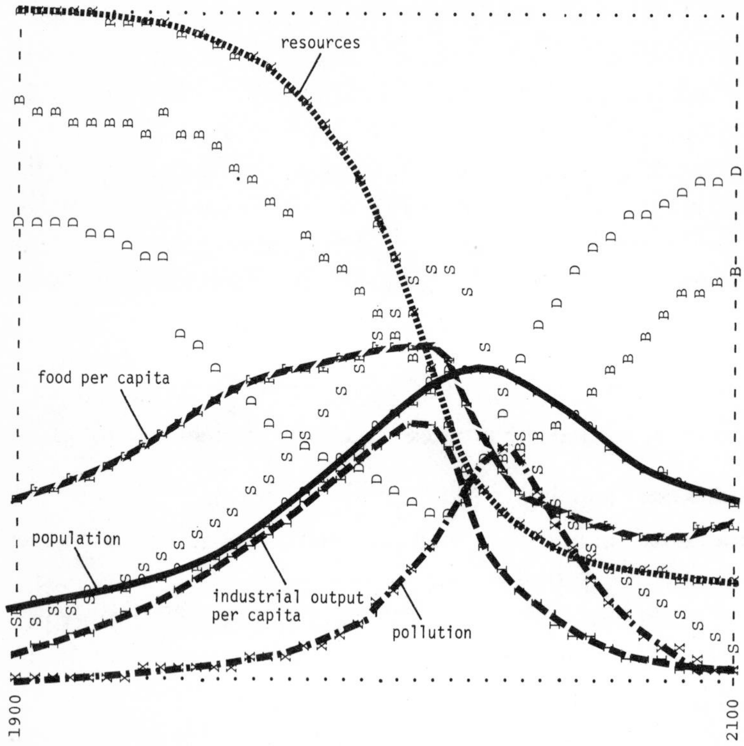

The "standard" world model run assumes no major change in the physical, economic, or social relationships that have historically governed the development of the world system. All variables plotted here follow historical values from 1900 to 1970. Food, industrial output, and population grow exponentially until the rapidly diminishing resource base forces a slowdown in industrial growth. Because of natural delays in the system, both population and pollution continue to increase for some time after the peak of industrialization. Population growth is finally halted by a rise in the death rate due to decreased food and medical services.

mately known. The scales are, however, exactly equal in all the computer runs presented here, so results of different runs may be easily compared.

All levels in the model (population, capital, pollution, etc.) begin with 1900 values. From 1900 to 1970 the variables plotted in figure 35 (and numerous other variables included in the model but not plotted here) agree generally with their historical values to the extent that we know them. Population rises from 1.6 billion in 1900 to 3.5 billion in 1970. Although the birth rate declines gradually, the death rate falls more quickly, especially after 1940, and the rate of population growth increases. Industrial output, food, and services per capita increase exponentially. The resource base in 1970 is still about 95 percent of its 1900 value, but it declines dramatically thereafter, as population and industrial output continue to grow.

The behavior mode of the system shown in figure 35 is clearly that of overshoot and collapse. In this run the collapse occurs because of nonrenewable resource depletion. The industrial capital stock grows to a level that requires an enormous input of resources. In the very process of that growth it depletes a large fraction of the resource reserves available. As resource prices rise and mines are depleted, more and more capital must be used for obtaining resources, leaving less to be invested for future growth. Finally investment cannot keep up with depreciation, and the industrial base collapses, taking with it the service and agricultural systems, which have become dependent on industrial inputs (such as fertilizers, pesticides, hospital laboratories, computers, and especially energy for mechanization). For a short time the situation is especially serious because population, with the delays inherent in the age structure and the process of social adjustment, keeps rising. Population finally decreases when the death rate is driven upward by lack of food and health services.

The exact timing of these events is not meaningful, given the great aggregation and many uncertainties in the model. It is significant, however, that growth is stopped well before the year 2100. We have tried in every doubtful case to make the most optimistic estimate of unknown quantities, and we have also ignored discontinuous events such as wars or epidemics, which might act to bring an end to growth even sooner than our model would indicate. In other words, the model is biased to allow growth to continue longer than it probably can continue in the real world. *We can thus say with some confidence that, under the assumption of no major change in the present system, population and industrial growth will certainly stop within the next century, at the latest.*

The system shown in figure 35 collapses because of a resource crisis. What if our estimate of the global stock of resources is wrong? In figure 35 we assumed that in 1970 there was a 250-year supply of all resources, at 1970 usage rates. The static reserve index column of the resource table in chapter II will verify that this assumption is indeed optimistic. But let us be even more optimistic and assume that new discoveries or advances in technology can *double* the amount of resources economically available. A computer run under that assumption is shown in figure 36.

The overall behavior mode in figure 36—growth and collapse—is very similar to that in the standard run. Resources are still severely depleted, in spite of the doubled amount available, simply because a few years of exponential growth in industry are sufficient to consume those extra resources. Thus industrial output declines and food production again falls once capital-intensive agriculture becomes impossible. In this run industry grows sufficiently to overload the natural absorptive capacity

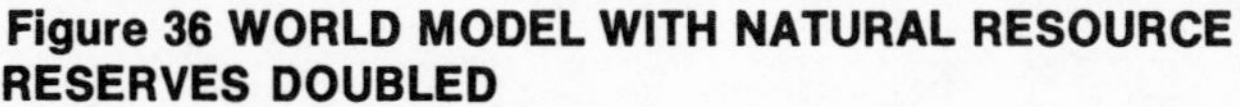

Figure 36 WORLD MODEL WITH NATURAL RESOURCE RESERVES DOUBLED

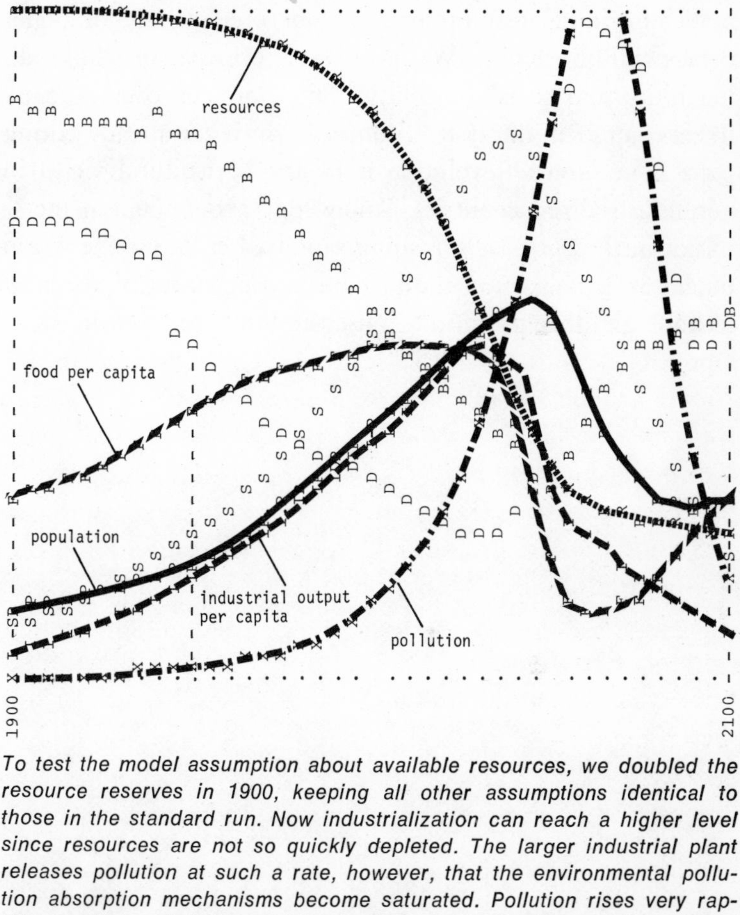

To test the model assumption about available resources, we doubled the resource reserves in 1900, keeping all other assumptions identical to those in the standard run. Now industrialization can reach a higher level since resources are not so quickly depleted. The larger industrial plant releases pollution at such a rate, however, that the environmental pollution absorption mechanisms become saturated. Pollution rises very rapidly, causing a slight increase in the death rate. Finally, a decline in food production results when the falling industrial output can no longer sustain capital-intensive agriculture. At the end of the run resources are severely depleted in spite of the doubled amount initially available.

of the environment. Thus the death rate rises from pollution and from lack of food.

Is the future of the world system bound to be growth and then collapse into a dismal, depleted existence? Only if we make the initial assumption that our present way of doing things will not change. We have ample evidence of mankind's ingenuity and social flexibility. There are, of course, many likely changes in the system, some of which are already taking place. The Green Revolution is raising agricultural yields in nonindustrialized countries. Knowledge about modern methods of birth control is spreading rapidly. Let us use the world model as a tool to test the possible consequences of the new technologies that promise to raise the limits to growth.

CHAPTER IV

TECHNOLOGY AND THE LIMITS TO GROWTH

Towards what ultimate point is society tending by its industrial progress? When the progress ceases, in what condition are we to expect that it will leave mankind?

JOHN STUART MILL, 1857

Although the history of human effort contains numerous incidents of mankind's failure to live within physical limits, it is success in overcoming limits that forms the cultural tradition of many dominant people in today's world. Over the past three hundred years, mankind has compiled an impressive record of pushing back the apparent limits to population and economic growth by a series of spectacular technological advances. Since the recent history of a large part of human society has been so continuously successful, it is quite natural that many people expect technological breakthroughs to go on raising physical ceilings indefinitely. These people speak about the future with resounding technological optimism.

> There are no substantial limits in sight either in raw materials or in energy that alterations in the price structure, product substitution, anticipated gains in technology and pollution control cannot be expected to solve.[35]

> Given the present capacity of the earth for food production, and the potential for additional food production if modern technology were more fully employed, the human race clearly has within its grasp the capacity to chase hunger from the earth—within a matter of a decade or two.[36]

> Humanity's mastery of vast, inanimate, inexhaustible energy sources and the accelerated doing more with less of sea, air, and space technology has proven Malthus to be wrong. Comprehensive physical and economic success for humanity may now be accomplished in one-fourth of a century.[37]

Can statements like these be reconciled with the evidence for the limits to growth we have discussed here? Will new technologies alter the tendency of the world system to grow and collapse? Before accepting or rejecting these optimistic views of a future based on technological solutions to mankind's problems, one would like to know more about the global impact of new technologies, in the short term and the long term, and in all five interlocking sectors of the population-capital system.

TECHNOLOGY IN THE WORLD MODEL

There is no single variable called "technology" in the world model. We have not found it possible to aggregate and generalize the dynamic implications of technological development because different technologies arise from and influence quite different sectors of the model. Birth control pills, high-yield grains, television, and off-shore oil-drilling rigs can all be considered technological developments, but each plays a distinct role in altering the behavior of the world system. Therefore we must represent each proposed technology separately in the model, considering carefully how it might affect each of the assumptions we have made about the model elements. In this section we shall present some examples of this approach to global, long-term "technology assessment."

Energy and resources

The technology of controlled nuclear fission has already lifted the impending limit of fossil fuel resources. It is also possible that the advent of fast breeder reactors and perhaps even fusion nuclear reactors will considerably extend the lifetime of fissionable fuels, such as uranium. Does this mean that man has mastered "vast, inanimate, inexhaustible energy sources" that will release unlimited raw materials for his industrial plants? What will be the effect of increasing use of nuclear power on resource availability in the world system?

Some experts believe that abundant energy resources will enable mankind to discover and utilize otherwise inaccessible materials (in the sea bed, for example); to process poorer ores, even down to common rock; and to recycle solid waste and reclaim the metals it contains. Although this is a common belief, it is by no means a universal one, as the following quotation by geologist Thomas Lovering indicates.

> Cheaper energy, in fact, would little reduce the total costs (chiefly capital and labor) required for mining and processing rock. The enormous quantities of unusable waste produced for each unit of metal in ordinary granite (in a ratio of at least 2,000 to 1) are more easily disposed of on a blueprint than in the field. . . . To recover minerals sought, the rock must be shattered by explosives, drilled for input and recovery wells, and flooded with solutions containing special extractive chemicals. Provision must then be made to avoid the loss of solutions and the consequent contamination of groundwater and surface water. These operations will not be obviated by nuclear power.[38]

Figure 37 WORLD MODEL WITH "UNLIMITED" RESOURCES

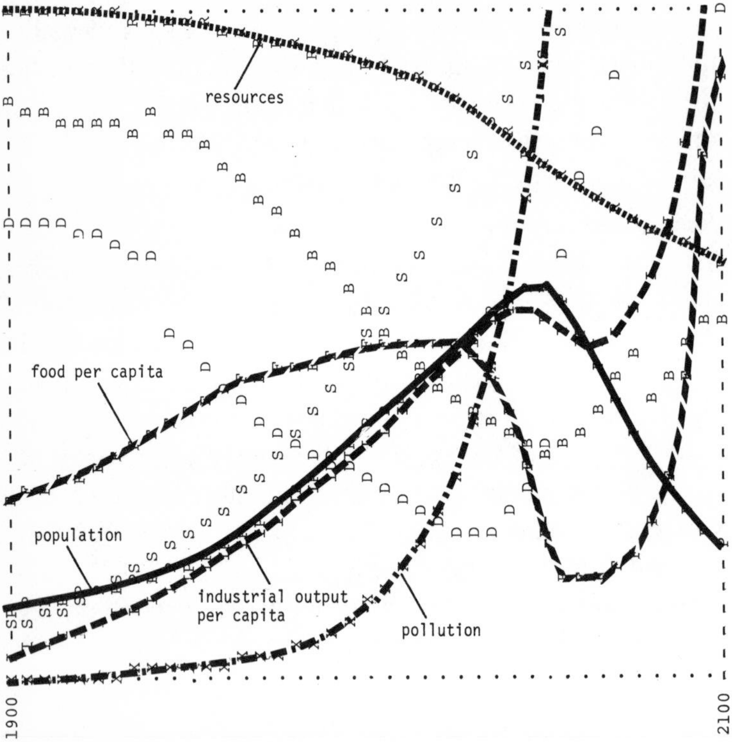

The problem of resource depletion in the world model system is eliminated by two assumptions: first, that "unlimited" nuclear power will double the resource reserves that can be exploited and, second, that nuclear energy will make extensive programs of recycling and substitution possible. If these changes are the only ones introduced in the system, growth is stopped by rising pollution.

Let us assume, however, that the technological optimists are correct and that nuclear energy will solve the resource problems of the world. The result of including that assumption in the world model is shown in figure 37. To express the possibility of utilizing lower grade ore or mining the seabed, we have doubled the total amount of resources available, as in figure 36. We have also assumed that, starting in 1975, programs of reclamation and recycling will reduce the input of virgin resources needed per unit of industrial output to only one-fourth of the amount used today. Both of these assumptions are, admittedly, more optimistic than realistic.

In figure 37 resource shortages indeed do not occur. Population growth is stopped by rising pollution. The absence of any constraint from resources allows industrial output and services to rise slightly higher than in figure 36 before they fall. Population reaches about the same peak level as it did in figure 36.

"Unlimited" resources thus do not appear to be the key to sustaining growth in the world system. Apparently the economic impetus such resource availability provides must be accompanied by curbs on pollution if a collapse of the world system is to be avoided.

Pollution control

We assumed in figure 37 that the advent of nuclear power neither increased nor decreased the average amount of pollution generated per unit of industrial output. The ecological impact of nuclear power is not yet clear. While some by-products of fossil fuel consumption, such as CO_2 and sulfur dioxide, will be decreased, radioactive by-products will be increased. Resource recycling will certainly decrease pollution from solid waste and from some toxic metals. However, a changeover to nuclear power will probably have little effect on most other kinds of pollution, including by-products of most manufacturing processes, thermal pollution, and pollution arising from agricultural practices.

Figure 38 COST OF POLLUTION REDUCTION

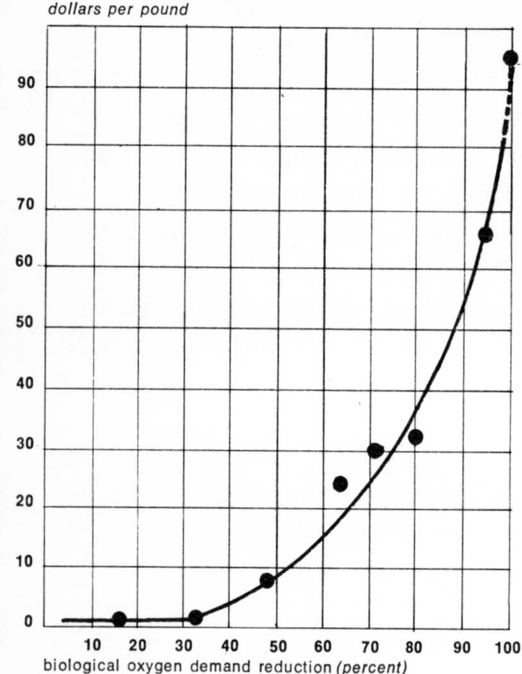

Incremental cost of reducing organic wastes from a 2,700-ton-per-day beet sugar plant rises steeply as emission standards approach complete purity. Reduction of biological oxygen demand (a measure of the oxygen required to decompose wastes) costs less than $1 a pound up to 30 percent reduction. Reduction beyond 65 percent requires more than $20 for each additional pound removed, and at 95 percent reduction, each pound removed costs $60.

SOURCE: *Second Annual Report of the Council on Environmental Quality* (Washington, DC: Government Printing Office, 1971).

It is likely, however, that a world society with readily available nuclear power would be able to control industrial pollution generation by technological means. Pollution control devices are already being developed and installed on a large scale in industrialized areas. How would the model behavior be changed if a policy of strict pollution control were instituted in, say, 1975?

Strict pollution control does not necessarily mean *total* pollution control. It is impossible to eliminate all pollution because of both technological and economic constraints. Economically, the cost of pollution control soars as emission standards become more severe. Figure 38 shows the cost of reducing water pollution from a sugar-processing plant as a function of organic wastes removed. If *no* organic wastes were allowed to leave the plant, the cost would be 100 times greater than if only 30 percent of the wastes were removed from the effluent. Table 6 below shows a similar trend in the projected costs of reducing air pollution in a US city.[39]

In figure 39 the world model output is plotted assuming *both* the reduction in resource depletion of figure 37 *and* a reduction in pollution generation from all sources by a factor of four,

Table 6 COST OF REDUCING AIR POLLUTION IN A US CITY

Percent reduction in SO_2	*Percent reduction in particulates*	*Projected cost*
5	22	$ 50,000
42	66	7,500,000
48	69	26,000,000

starting in 1975. Reduction to less than one-fourth of the present rate of pollution generation is probably unrealistic because of cost, and because of the difficulty of eliminating some kinds of pollution, such as thermal pollution and radioisotopes from nuclear power generation, fertilizer runoff, and asbestos particles from brake linings. We assume that such a sharp reduc-

Figure 39 WORLD MODEL WITH "UNLIMITED" RESOURCES AND POLLUTION CONTROLS

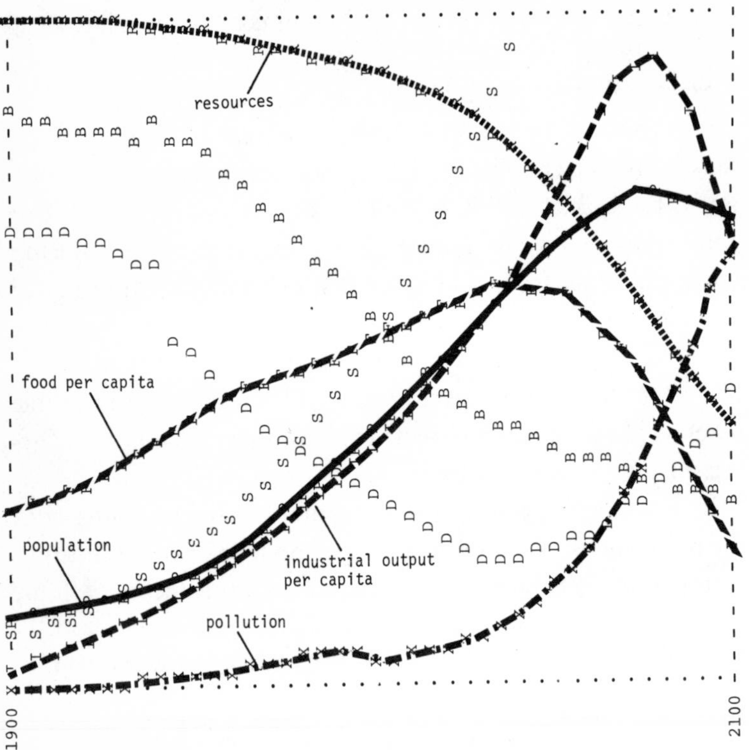

A further technological improvement is added to the world model in 1975 to avoid the resource depletion and pollution problems of previous model runs. Here we assume that pollution generation per unit of industrial and agricultural output can be reduced to one-fourth of its 1970 value. Resource policies are the same as those in figure 37. These changes allow population and industry to grow until the limit of arable land is reached. Food per capita declines, and industrial growth is also slowed as capital is diverted to food production.

tion in pollution generation could occur globally and quickly for purposes of experimentation with the model, not because we believe it is politically feasible, given our present institutions.

As figure 39 shows, the pollution control policy is indeed successful in reducing the pollution crisis of the previous run. Both population and industrial output per person rise well beyond their peak values in figure 37, and yet resource depletion and pollution never become serious problems. The overshoot mode is still operative, however, and the collapse comes about this time primarily from food shortage.

As long as industrial output is rising in figure 39, the yield from each hectare of land continues to rise (up to a maximum of ten times the average yield in 1900) and new land is developed. At the same time, however, some arable land is taken for urban-industrial use, and some land is eroded, especially by highly capitalized agricultural practices. Eventually the limit of arable land is reached. After that point, as population continues to rise, food per capita decreases. As the food shortage becomes apparent, industrial output is diverted into agricultural capital to increase land yields. Less capital is available for investment, and finally the industrial output per capita begins to fall. As food per capita sinks to the subsistence level, the death rate begins to increase, bringing an end to population growth.

Increased food yield and birth control

The problem in figure 39 could be viewed either as too little food or as too many people. The technological response to the first situation would be to produce more food, perhaps by some further extension of the principles of the Green Revolution. (The development of the new, high-yield grain varieties which constitutes the Green Revolution has been included in the original model equations.) The technological solution to the second problem would be to provide better methods of birth

Figure 40 WORLD MODEL WITH "UNLIMITED" RESOURCES, POLLUTION CONTROLS, AND INCREASED AGRICULTURAL PRODUCTIVITY

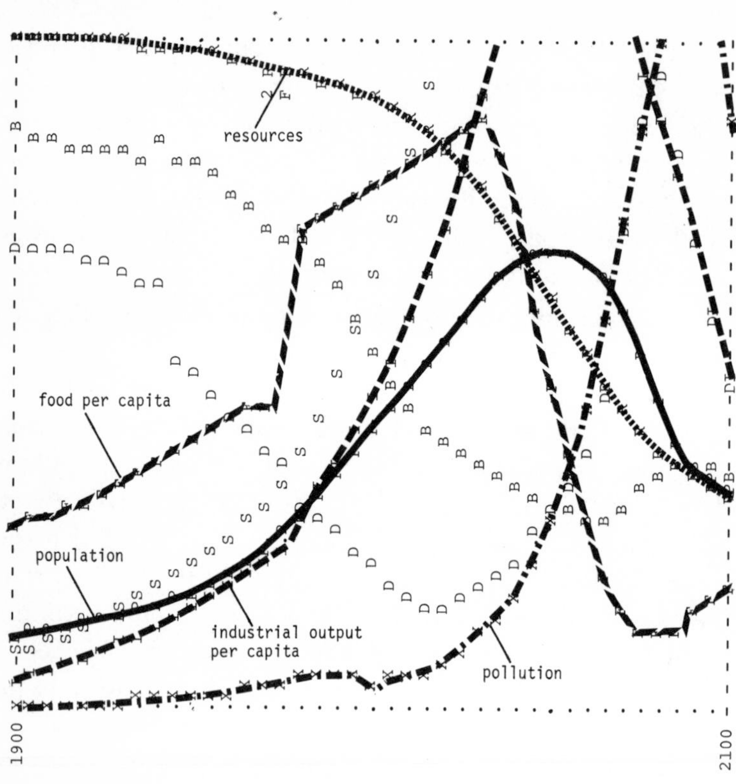

To avoid the food crisis of the previous model run, average land yield is doubled in 1975 in addition to the pollution and resource policies of previous figures. The combination of these three policies removes so many constraints to growth that population and industry reach very high levels. Although each unit of industrial production generates much less pollution, total production rises enough to create a pollution crisis. In addition, intensive use of land leads to soil erosion and food shortages.

control. The results of these two changes, instituted in 1975 along with the changes in resource use and pollution generation we have already discussed, are shown both separately and simultaneously in figures 40, 41, and 42.

In figure 40 we assume that the normal yield per hectare of

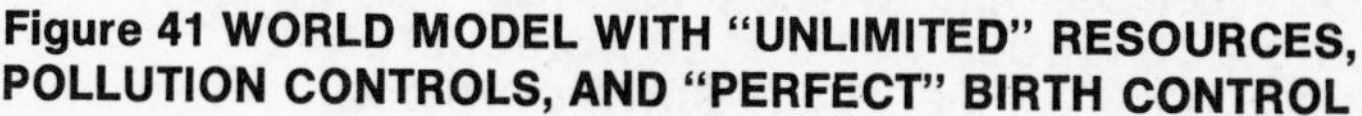

Figure 41 WORLD MODEL WITH "UNLIMITED" RESOURCES, POLLUTION CONTROLS, AND "PERFECT" BIRTH CONTROL

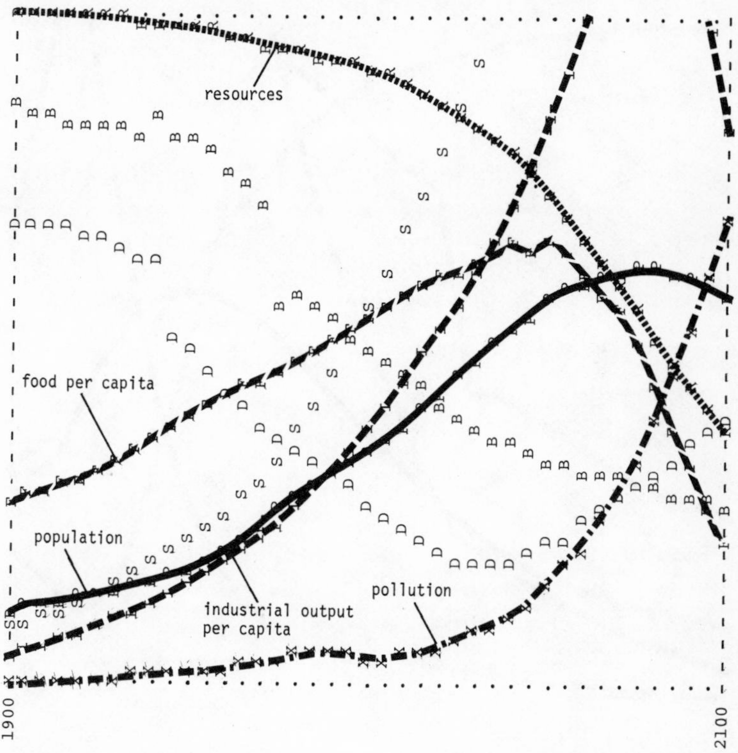

Instead of an increase in food production, an increase in birth control effectiveness is tested as a policy to avert the food problem. Since the birth control is voluntary and does not involve any value changes, population continues to grow, but more slowly than it did in figure 39. Nevertheless, the food crisis is postponed for only a decade or two.

all the world's land can be further increased by a factor of two. The result is an enormous increase in food, industrial output, and services per capita. Average industrial output per person for all the world's people becomes nearly equal to the 1970 US level, but only briefly. Although a strict pollution control policy is still in effect, so that pollution per unit of output is

Figure 42 WORLD MODEL WITH "UNLIMITED" RESOURCES, POLLUTION CONTROLS, INCREASED AGRICULTURAL PRODUCTIVITY, AND "PERFECT" BIRTH CONTROL

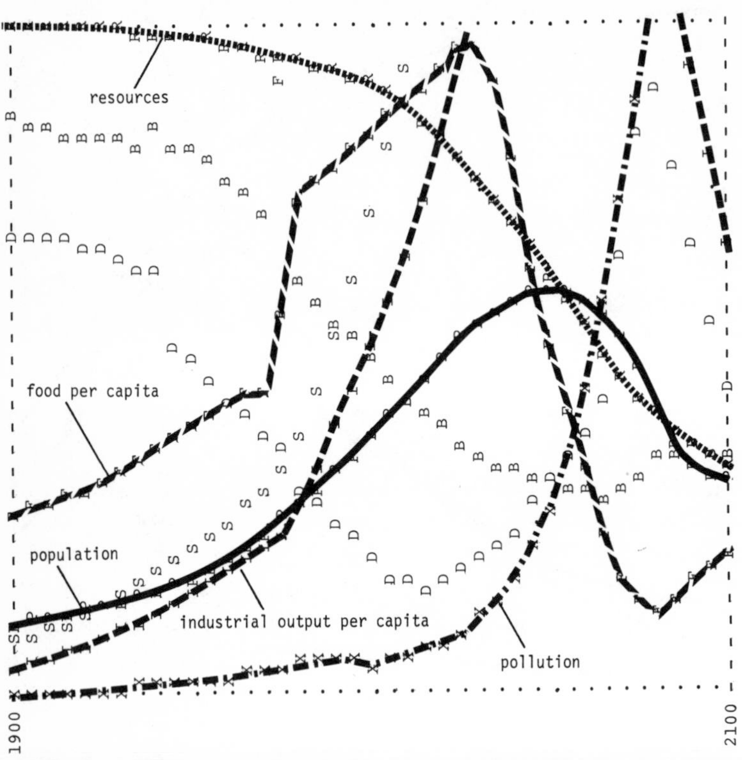

Four simultaneous technological policies are introduced in the world model in an attempt to avoid the growth-and-collapse behavior of previous runs. Resources are fully exploited, and 75 percent of those used are recycled. Pollution generation is reduced to one-fourth of its 1970 value. Land yields are doubled, and effective methods of birth control are made available to the world population. The result is a temporary achievement of a world average income per capita that reaches nearly the present US level. Finally, though, industrial growth is halted, and the death rate rises as resources are depleted, pollution accumulates, and food production declines.

reduced by a factor of four, industry grows so quickly that soon it is producing four times as much output. Thus the level of pollution rises in spite of the pollution control policy, and mortality increases. In addition, intensive agricultural practices cause soil erosion and lead to food shortages.

Figure 41 shows the alternate technological policy—perfect birth control, practiced voluntarily, starting in 1975. The result is not to stop population growth entirely because such a policy prevents only the births of *unwanted* children. The birth rate does decrease markedly, however, and the population grows more slowly than it did in figures 39 and 40. In this run growth is stopped by a food crisis occurring about 20 years later than in figure 39.

In figure 42 we apply increased land yield and perfect birth control simultaneously. Here we are utilizing a technological policy in every sector of the world model to circumvent in some way the various limits to growth. The model system is producing nuclear power, recycling resources, and mining the most remote reserves; withholding as many pollutants as possible; pushing yields from the land to undreamed-of heights; and producing only children who are actively wanted by their parents. The result is still an end to growth before the year 2100. In this case growth is stopped by three simultaneous crises. Overuse of land leads to erosion, and food production drops. Resources are severely depleted by a prosperous world population (but not as prosperous as the present US population). Pollution rises, causing a slight rise in the death rate. The application of technological solutions alone has prolonged the period of population and industrial growth, but it has not removed the ultimate limits to that growth.

The overshoot mode

Given the many approximations and limitations of the world model, there is no point in dwelling glumly on the series of catastrophes it tends to generate. We shall emphasize just one more time that none of these computer outputs is a prediction. We would not expect the real world to behave like the world model in any of the graphs we have shown, especially in the collapse modes. The model contains dynamic statements about only the physical aspects of man's activities. It assumes that social variables—income distribution, attitudes about family size, choices among goods, services, and food—will continue to follow the same patterns they have followed throughout the world in recent history. These patterns, and the human values they represent, were all established in the growth phase of our civilization. They would certainly be greatly revised as population and income began to decrease. Since we find it difficult to imagine what new forms of human societal behavior might emerge and how quickly they would emerge under collapse conditions, we have not attempted to model such social changes. What validity our model has holds up only to the point in each output graph at which growth comes to an end and collapse begins.

Although we have many reservations about the approximations and simplifications in the present world model, it has led us to one conclusion that appears to be justified under all the assumptions we have tested so far. *The basic behavior mode of the world system is exponential growth of population and capital, followed by collapse.* As we have shown in the model runs presented here, this behavior mode occurs if we assume no change in the present system or if we assume any number of technological changes in the system.

The unspoken assumption behind all of the model runs we have presented in this chapter is that population and capital growth should be allowed to continue until they reach some "natural" limit. This assumption also appears to be a basic part of the human value system currently operational in the real world. Whenever we incorporate this value into the model, the result is that the growing system rises above its ultimate limit and then collapses. When we introduce technological developments that successfully lift some restraint to growth or avoid some collapse, the system simply grows to another limit, temporarily surpasses it, and falls back. Given that first assumption, that population and capital growth should not be deliberately limited but should be left to "seek their own levels," we have not been able to find a set of policies that avoids the collapse mode of behavior.

It is not really difficult to understand how the collapse mode comes about. Everywhere in the web of interlocking feedback loops that constitutes the world system we have found it necessary to represent the real-world situation by introducing time delays between causes and their ultimate effects. These are natural delays that cannot be controlled by technological means. They include, for example, the delay of about fifteen years between the birth of a baby and the time that baby can first reproduce itself. The time delay inherent in the aging of a population introduces a certain unavoidable lag in the ability of the population to respond through the birth rate to changing conditions. Another delay occurs between the time a pollutant is released into the environment and the time it has a measurable influence on human health. This delay includes the passage of the pollutant through air or rivers or soil and into the food chain, and also the time from human ingestion or absorption of the pollutant until clinical symptoms appear. This second delay may be as long as 20 years in the case of some carcinogens. Other delays occur because capital cannot be transferred instantly from one sector to another to meet changing demands, because new capital and land can only be produced or developed gradually, and because pollution can only slowly be dispersed or metabolized into harmless forms.

Delays in a dynamic system have serious effects only if the system itself is undergoing rapid changes. Perhaps a simple example will clarify that statement. When you drive a car there is a very short, unavoidable delay between your perception of the road in front of you and your reaction to it. There is a longer delay between your action on the accelerator or brakes and the car's response to that action. You have learned to deal with those delays. You know that, because of the delays, it is unsafe to drive too fast. If you do, you will certainly experience the overshoot and collapse mode, sooner or later. If you were blindfolded and had to drive on the instructions of a front-seat passenger, the delay between perception and action would be considerably lengthened. The only safe way to handle the extended delay would be to slow down. If you tried to drive your normal speed, or if you tried to accelerate continuously (as in exponential growth), the result would be disastrous.

In exactly the same way, the delays in the feedback loops of the world system would be no problem if the system were growing very slowly or not at all. Under those conditions any new action or policy could be instituted gradually, and the changes could work their way through the delays to feed back on every part of the system before some other action or policy would have to be introduced. Under conditions of rapid growth, however, the system is forced into new policies and actions long before the results of old policies and actions can be properly assessed. The situation is even worse when the growth is exponential and the system is changing ever more rapidly.

Thus population and capital, driven by exponential growth, not only reach their limits, but temporarily shoot beyond them before the rest of the system, with its inherent delays, reacts to stop growth. Pollution generated in exponentially increasing amounts can rise past the danger point, because the danger point is first perceived years after the offending pollution was released. A rapidly growing industrial system can build up a capital base dependent on a given resource and then discover that the exponentially shrinking resource reserves cannot support it. Because of delays in the age structure, a population will continue to grow for as long as 70 years, even after average fertility has dropped below the replacement level (an average of two children for each married couple).

TECHNOLOGY IN THE REAL WORLD

The hopes of the technological optimists center on the ability of technology to remove or extend the limits to growth of population and capital. We have shown that in the world model the application of technology to apparent problems of resource depletion or pollution or food shortage has no impact on the *essential* problem, which is exponential growth in a finite and complex system. Our attempts to use even the most optimistic estimates of the benefits of technology in the model did not prevent the ultimate decline of population and industry, and in fact did not in any case postpone the collapse beyond the year 2100. Before we go on in the next chapter to test other policies, which are not technological, let us extend our discussion of technological solutions to some aspects of technology that could not be included in the world model.

Technological side-effects

Dr. Garrett Hardin has defined side-effects as "effects which I hadn't foreseen or don't want to think about."[40] He has suggested that, since such effects are actually inseparable from the principal effect, they should not be labeled *side*-effects at all. Every new technology has side-effects, of course, and one of the main purposes of model-building is to anticipate those effects. The model runs in this chapter have shown some of the side-effects of various technologies on the world's physical and economic systems. Unfortunately the model does not indicate, at this stage, the *social* side-effects of new technologies. These effects are often the most important in terms of the influence of a technology on people's lives.

A recent example of social side-effects from a successful new technology appeared as the Green Revolution was introduced to the agrarian societies of the world. The Green Revolution—the utilization of new seed varieties, combined with fertilizers and pesticides—was designed to be a technological solution to the world's food problems. The planners of this new agricultural technology foresaw some of the social problems it might raise in traditional cultures. The Green Revolution was intended not only to produce more food but to be labor-intensive—to provide jobs and not to require large amounts of capital. In some areas of the world, such as the Indian Punjab, the Green Revolution has indeed increased the number of agricultural jobs faster than the rate of growth of the total population. In the East Punjab there was a real wage increase of 16 percent from 1963 to 1968.[41]

The principal, or intended, effect of the Green Revolution—increased food production—seems to have been achieved. Unfortunately the social side-effects have not been entirely beneficial in most regions where the new seed varieties have been introduced. The Indian Punjab had, before the Green Revolution, a remarkably equitable system of land distribution. The more common pattern in the nonindustrialized world is a wide range in land ownership, with most people working very small farms and a few people in possession of the vast majority of the land.

Where these conditions of economic inequality already exist, the Green Revolution tends to cause widening inequality. Large farmers generally adopt the new methods first. They have the capital to do so and can afford to take the risk. Although the new seed varieties do not require tractor mechanization, they provide much economic incentive for mechanization, especially where multiple cropping requires a quick harvest and replanting. On large farms, simple economic considerations lead almost inevitably to the use of labor-displacing machinery and to the purchase of still more land.[42] The ultimate effects of this socio-economic positive feedback loop are agricultural unemployment, increased migration to the city, and perhaps even increased malnutrition, since the poor and unemployed do not have the means to buy the newly produced food.

A specific example of the social side-effects of the Green Revolution in an area where land is unequally distributed is described below.

> A landless laborer's income in West Pakistan today is still just about what it was five years ago, less than $100 a year. In contrast, one landlord with a 1,500-acre wheat farm told me when I was in Pakistan this winter that he had cleared a net profit of more than $100,000 on his last harvest.[43]

Statistics from Mexico, where the Green Revolution began

in the 1940's, provide another example. From 1940 to 1960 the average growth rate of agricultural production in Mexico was 5 percent per year. From 1950 to 1960, however, the average number of days worked by a landless laborer fell from 194 to 100, and his real income decreased from $68 to $56. Eighty percent of the increased agricultural production came from only 3 percent of the farms.[44]

These unexpected social side-effects do not imply that the technology of the Green Revolution was unsuccessful. They do imply that social side-effects must be anticipated and forestalled *before* the large-scale introduction of a new technology.

> As agriculture emerges from its traditional subsistence state to modern commercial farming . . . it becomes progressively more important to ensure that adequate rewards accrue directly to the man who tills the soil. Indeed, it is hard to see how there can be any meaningful modernization of food production in Latin America and Africa south of the Sahara unless land is registered, deeded, and distributed more equitably.[45]

Such preparation for technological change requires, at the very least, a great deal of time. Every change in the normal way of doing things requires an adjustment time, while the population, consciously or unconsciously, restructures its social system to accommodate the change. While technology can change rapidly, political and social institutions generally change very slowly. Furthermore, they almost never change *in anticipation* of a social need, but only in response to one.

We have already mentioned the dynamic effect of physical delays in the world model. We must also keep in mind the presence of social delays—the delays necessary to allow society to absorb or to prepare for a change. Most delays, physical or social, reduce the stability of the world system and increase the likelihood of the overshoot mode. The social delays, like the physical ones, are becoming increasingly more critical because the processes of exponential growth are creating additional pressures at a faster and faster rate. The world population grew from 1 billion to 2 billion over a period of more than one hundred years. The third billion was added in 30 years and the world's population has had less than 20 years to prepare for its fourth billion. The fifth, sixth, and perhaps even seventh billions may arrive before the year 2000, less than 30 years from now. Although the rate of technological change has so far managed to keep up with this accelerated pace, mankind has made virtually no new discoveries to increase the rate of social (political, ethical, and cultural) change.

Problems with no technical solutions

When the cities of America were new, they grew rapidly. Land was abundant and cheap, new buildings rose continuously, and the population and economic output of urban regions increased. Eventually, however, all the land in the city center was filled. A physical limit had been reached, threatening to stop population and economic growth in that section of the city. The technological answer was the development of skyscrapers and elevators, which essentially removed the constraint of land area as a factor in suppressing growth. The central city added more people and more businesses. Then a new constraint appeared. Goods and workers could not move in and out of the dense center city quickly enough. Again the solution was technological. A network of expressways, mass transit systems, and helicopter ports on the tops of the tallest buildings was constructed. The transportation limit was overcome, the buildings grew taller, the population increased.

Now most of the larger US cities have stopped growing. (Of the ten largest, five—New York, Chicago, Philadelphia, Detroit, and Baltimore—decreased in population from 1960 to 1970. Washington, DC, showed no change. Los Angeles, Houston, Dallas, and Indianapolis continued to grow, at least in part by annexing additional land.)[46] The wealthier people, who have an economic choice, are moving to the ever-expanding ring of suburbs around the cities. The central areas are characterized by noise, pollution, crime, drug addiction, poverty, labor strikes, and breakdown of social services. The quality of life in the city core has declined. Growth has been stopped in part by problems with no technical solutions.

A technical solution may be defined as "one that requires a change only in the techniques of the natural sciences, demanding little or nothing in the way of change in human values or ideas of morality."[47] Numerous problems today have no technical solutions. Examples are the nuclear arms race, racial tensions, and unemployment. Even if society's technological progress fulfills all expectations, it may very well be a problem with no technical solution, or the interaction of several such problems, that finally brings an end to population and capital growth.

A choice of limits

Applying technology to the natural pressures that the environment exerts against any growth process has been so successful in the past that a whole culture has evolved around the principle of fighting against limits rather than learning to live with them. This culture has been reinforced by the apparent immensity of the earth and its resources and by the relative smallness of man and his activities.

But the relationship between the earth's limits and man's activities is changing. The exponential growth curves are adding millions of people and billions of tons of pollutants to the ecosystem each year. Even the ocean, which once appeared virtually inexhaustible, is losing species after species of its commercially useful animals. Recent FAO statistics indicate that the total catch of the world's fisheries decreased in 1969 for the first time since 1950, in spite of more mechanized and intensive fishing practices. (Among commercial species becoming increasingly scarce are Scandinavian herring, menhaden, and Atlantic cod.)[48]

Yet man does not seem to learn by running into the earth's obvious limits. The story of the whaling industry (shown in figure 43) demonstrates, for one small system, the ultimate result of the attempt to grow forever in a limited environment. Whalers have systematically reached one limit after another and have attempted to overcome each one by increases in power and technology. As a result, they have wiped out one species after another. The outcome of this particular grow-forever policy can only be the final extinction of both whales and whalers. The alternative policy is the imposition of a *man-determined limit* on the number of whales taken each year, set so that the whale population is maintained at a steady-state level. The self-imposed limit on whaling would be an unpleasant pressure that would prevent the growth of the industry. But perhaps it would be preferable to the gradual disappearance of both whales and whaling industry.

The basic choice that faces the whaling industry is the same one that faces any society trying to overcome a natural limit with a new technology. *Is it better to try to live within that limit by accepting a self-imposed restriction on growth? Or*

Figure 43 MODERN WHALING

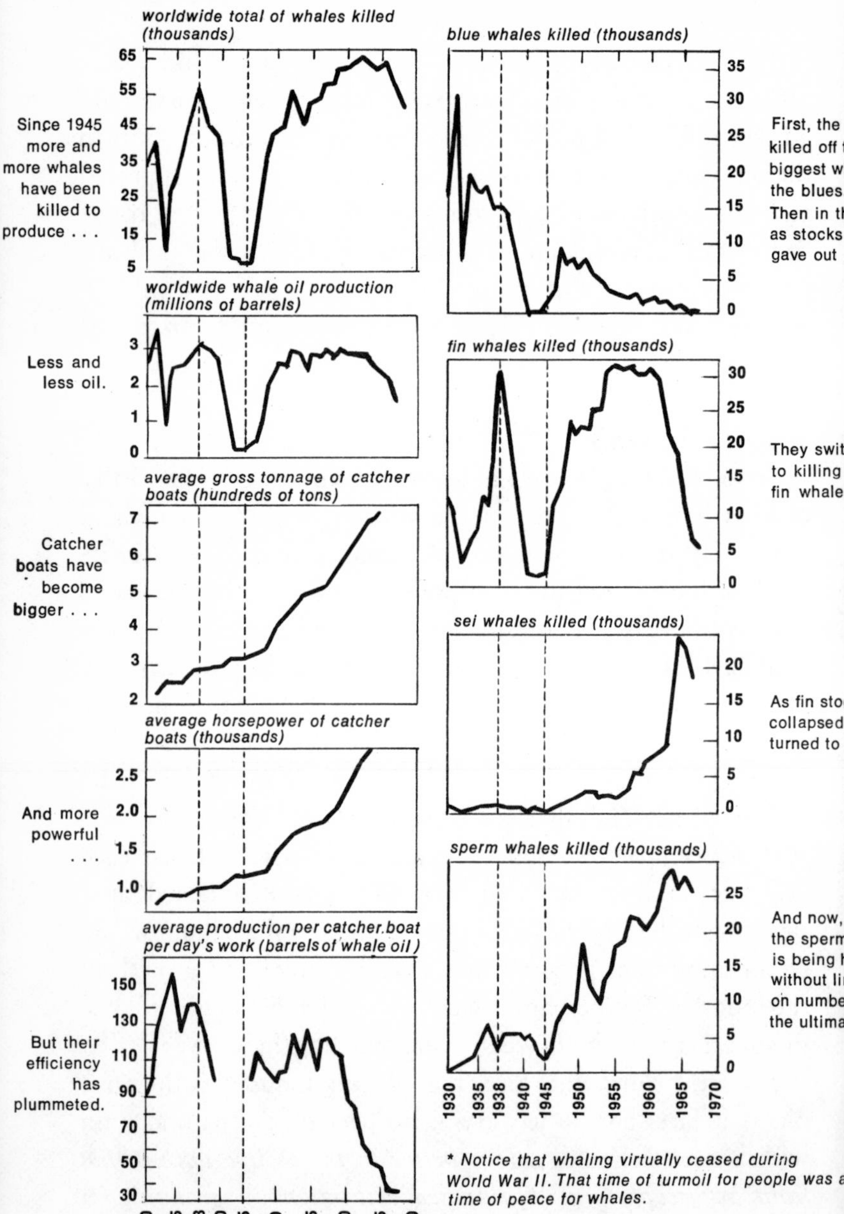

* Notice that whaling virtually ceased during World War II. That time of turmoil for people was a time of peace for whales.

As wild herds of whales have been destroyed, finding the survivors has become more difficult and has required more effort. As larger whales are killed off, smaller species are exploited to keep the industry alive. Since there have never been species limits, however, large whales are always taken wherever and whenever encountered. Thus small whales are used to subsidize the extermination of large ones.

SOURCE: Roger Payne, "Among Wild Whales," in *The New York Zoological Society Newsletter,* November 1968.

is it preferable to go on growing until some other natural limit arises, in the hope that at that time another technological leap will allow growth to continue still longer? For the last several hundred years human society has followed the second course so consistently and successfully that the first choice has been all but forgotten.

There may be much disagreement with the statement that population and capital growth must stop *soon.* But virtually no one will argue that material growth on this planet can go on forever. At this point in man's history, the choice posed above is still available in almost every sphere of human activity. Man can still choose his limits and stop when he pleases by weakening some of the strong pressures that cause capital and population growth, or by instituting counterpressures, or both. Such counterpressures will probably not be entirely pleasant. They will certainly involve profound changes in the social and economic structures that have been deeply impressed into human culture by centuries of growth. The alternative is to wait until the price of technology becomes more than society can pay, or until the side-effects of technology suppress growth themselves, or until problems arise that have no technical solutions. At any of those points the choice of limits will be gone. Growth will be stopped by pressures that are not of human choosing, and that, as the world model suggests, may be very much worse than those which society might choose for itself.

We have felt it necessary to dwell so long on an analysis of technology here because we have found that technological optimism is the most common and the most dangerous reaction to our findings from the world model. Technology can relieve the symptoms of a problem without affecting the underlying causes. Faith in technology as the ultimate solution to all problems can thus divert our attention from the most fundamental problem—the problem of growth in a finite system—and prevent us from taking effective action to solve it.

On the other hand, our intent is certainly not to brand technology as evil or futile or unnecessary. We are technologists ourselves, working in a technological institution. We strongly believe, as we shall point out in the following chapter, that many of the technological developments mentioned here—recycling, pollution control devices, contraceptives—will be absolutely vital to the future of human society *if they are combined with deliberate checks on growth*. We would deplore an unreasoned rejection of the benefits of technology as strongly as we argue here against an unreasoned acceptance of them. Perhaps the best summary of our position is the motto of the Sierra Club: "Not blind opposition to progress, but opposition to blind progress."

We would hope that society will receive each new technological advance by establishing the answers to three questions *before* the technology is widely adopted. The questions are:

1. What will be the side-effects, both physical and social, if this development is introduced on a large scale?

2. What social changes will be necessary before this develop-

ment can be implemented properly, and how long will it take to achieve them?

3. If the development is fully successful and removes some natural limit to growth, what limit will the growing system meet next? Will society prefer its pressures to the ones this development is designed to remove?

Let us go on now to investigate nontechnical approaches for dealing with growth in a finite world.

CHAPTER V

THE STATE OF GLOBAL EQUILIBRIUM

Most persons think that a state in order to be happy ought to be large; but even if they are right, they have no idea of what is a large and what a small state. . . . To the size of states there is a limit, as there is to other things, plants, animals, implements; for none of these retain their natural power when they are too large or too small, but they either wholly lose their nature, or are spoiled.

ARISTOTLE, 322 B.C.

We have seen that positive feedback loops operating without any constraints generate exponential growth. In the world system two positive feedback loops are dominant now, producing exponential growth of population and of industrial capital.

In any finite system there must be constraints that can act to stop exponential growth. These constraints are negative feedback loops. The negative loops become stronger and stronger as growth approaches the ultimate limit, or carrying capacity, of the system's environment. Finally the negative loops balance or dominate the positive ones, and growth comes to an end. In the world system the negative feedback loops involve such processes as pollution of the environment, depletion of nonrenewable resources, and famine.

The delays inherent in the action of these negative loops tend to allow population and capital to overshoot their ultimately sustainable levels. The period of overshoot is wasteful of resources. It generally decreases the carrying capacity of the environment as well, intensifying the eventual decline in population and capital.

The growth-stopping pressures from negative feedback loops are already being felt in many parts of human society. The major societal responses to these pressures have been directed at the negative feedback loops themselves. Technological solutions, such as those discussed in chapter IV, have been devised to weaken the loops or to disguise the pressures they generate so that growth can continue. Such means may have some short-term effect in relieving pressures caused by growth, but in the long run they do nothing to prevent the overshoot and subsequent collapse of the system.

Another response to the problems created by growth would be to weaken the *positive* feedback loops that are generating the growth. Such a solution has almost never been acknowledged as legitimate by any modern society, and it has certainly never been effectively carried out. What kinds of policies would such a solution involve? What sort of world would result? There is almost no historical precedent for such an approach, and thus there is no alternative but to discuss it in terms of models—either mental models or formal, written models. How will the world model behave if we include in it some policy to control growth deliberately? Will such a policy change generate a "better" behavior mode?

Whenever we use words such as "better" and begin choosing among alternative model outputs, we, the experimenters, are inserting our own values and preferences into the modeling process. The values built into each causal relationship of the model are the real, operational values of the world to the degree that we can determine them. The values that cause us to rank computer outputs as "better" or "worse" are the personal values of the modeler or his audience. We have already asserted our own value system by rejecting the overshoot and collapse mode as undesirable. Now that we are seeking a "better" result, we must define our goal for the system as clearly as possible. We are searching for a model output that represents a world system that is:

1. sustainable without sudden and uncontrollable collapse; and

2. capable of satisfying the basic material requirements of all of its people.

Now let us see what policies will bring about such behavior in the world model.

DELIBERATE CONSTRAINTS ON GROWTH

You will recall that the positive feedback loop generating population growth involves the birth rate and all the socio-economic factors that influence the birth rate. It is counteracted by the negative loop of the death rate.

The overwhelming growth in world population caused by the positive birth-rate loop is a recent phenomenon, a result of mankind's very successful reduction of worldwide mortality. The controlling negative feedback loop has been weakened, allowing the positive loop to operate virtually without constraint. There are only two ways to restore the resulting imbalance. Either the birth rate must be brought down to equal the new, lower death rate, or the death rate must rise again. All of the "natural" constraints to population growth operate in the second way—they raise the death rate. Any society wishing to avoid that result must take deliberate action to control the positive feedback loop—to reduce the birth rate.

In a dynamic model it is a simple matter to counteract runaway positive feedback loops. For the moment let us suspend the requirement of political feasibility and use the model to test the physical, if not the social, implications of limiting population growth. We need only add to the model one more causal loop, connecting the birth rate and the death rate. In other words, we require that the number of babies born each year be equal to the expected number of deaths in the population that year. Thus the positive and negative feedback loops are exactly balanced. As the death rate decreases, because of better food and medical care, the birth rate will decrease

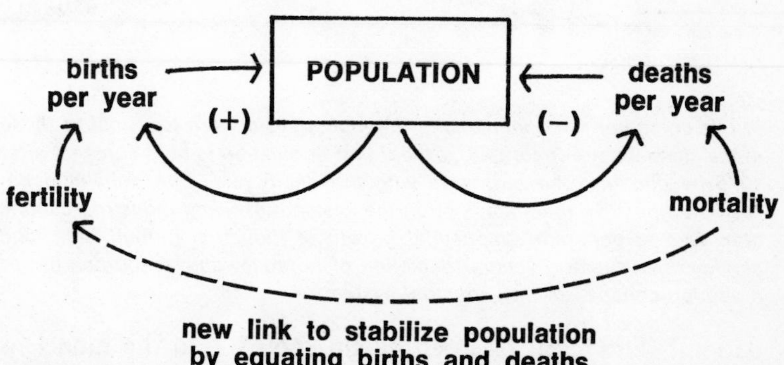

simultaneously. Such a requirement, which is as mathematically simple as it is socially complicated, is for our purposes an experimental device, not necessarily a political recommen-

Figure 44 WORLD MODEL WITH STABILIZED POPULATION

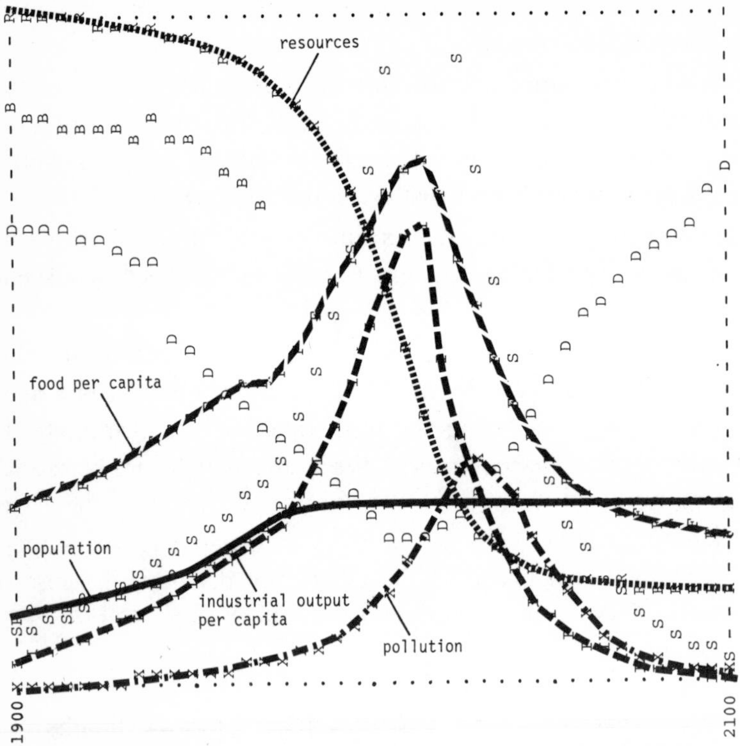

In this computer run conditions in the model system are identical to those in the standard run (figure 35), except that population is held constant after 1975 by equating the birth rate with the death rate. The remaining unrestricted positive feedback loop in the system, involving industrial capital, continues to generate exponential growth of industrial output, food, and services per capita Eventual depletion of nonrenewable resources brings a sudden collapse of the industrial system.

dation.* The result of inserting this policy into the model in 1975 is shown in figure 44.

---

* This suggestion for stabilizing population was originally proposed by Kenneth E. Boulding in *The Meaning of the 20th Century* (New York: Harper and Row, 1964).

In figure 44 the positive feedback loop of population growth is effectively balanced, and population remains constant. At first the birth and death rates are low. But there is still one unchecked positive feedback loop operating in the model—the one governing the growth of industrial capital. The gain around that loop increases when population is stabilized, resulting in a very rapid growth of income, food, and services per capita. That growth is soon stopped, however, by depletion of nonrenewable resources. The death rate then rises, but total population does not decline because of our requirement that birth rate equal death rate (clearly unrealistic here).

Apparently, if we want a stable system, it is not desirable to let even one of the two critical positive feedback loops generate uncontrolled growth. Stabilizing population alone is not sufficient to prevent overshoot and collapse; a similar run with constant capital and rising population shows that stabilizing capital alone is also not sufficient. What happens if we bring *both* positive feedback loops under control simultaneously? We can stabilize the capital stock in the model by requiring that the investment rate equal the depreciation rate, with an additional model link exactly analogous to the population-stabilizing one.

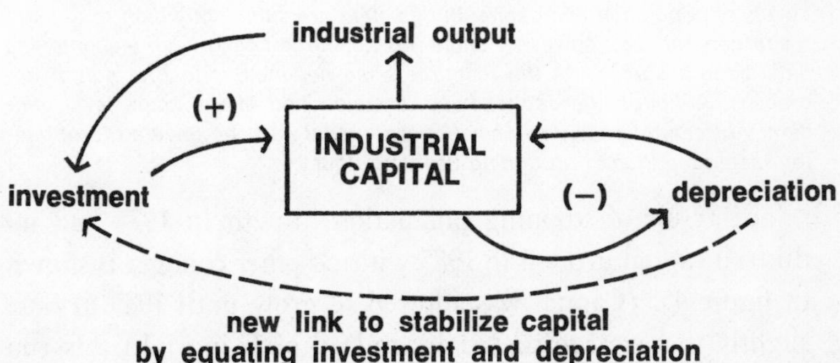

Figure 45 WORLD MODEL WITH STABILIZED POPULATION AND CAPITAL

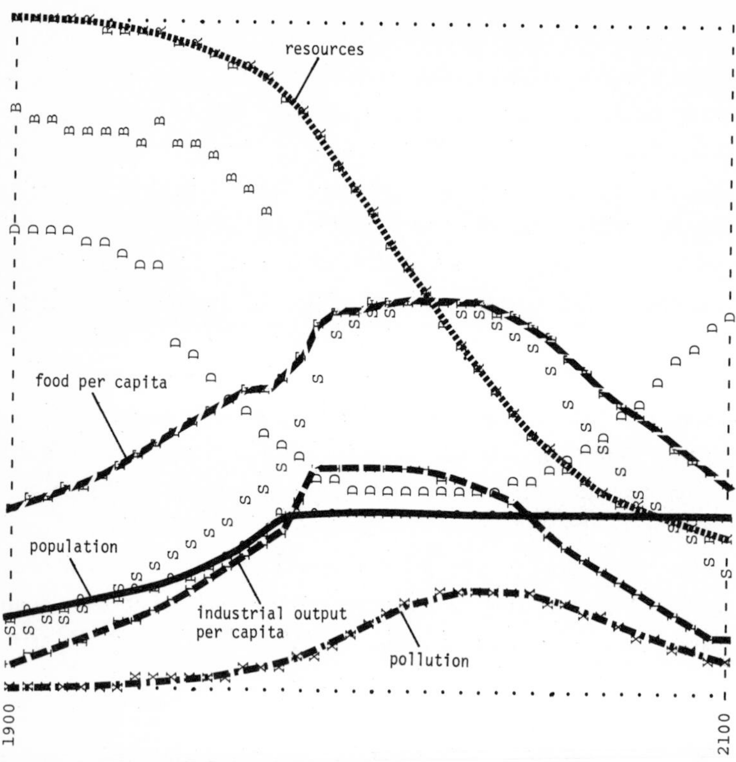

Restriction of capital growth, by requiring that capital investment equal depreciation, is added to the population stabilization policy of figure 44. Now that exponential growth is halted, a temporary stable state is attained. Levels of population and capital in this state are sufficiently high to deplete resources rapidly, however, since no resource-conserving technologies have been assumed. As the resource base declines, industrial output decreases. Although the capital base is maintained at the same level, efficiency of capital goes down since more capital must be devoted to obtaining resources than to producing usable output.

The result of stopping population growth in 1975 and industrial capital growth in 1985 with no other changes is shown in figure 45. (Capital was allowed to grow until 1985 to raise slightly the average material standard of living.) In this run the severe overshoot and collapse of figure 44 are prevented. Population and capital reach constant values at a relatively high level of food, industrial output, and services per person. Eventually, however, resource shortages reduce industrial output and the temporarily stable state degenerates.

What model assumptions will give us a combination of a decent living standard with somewhat greater stability than that attained in figure 45? We can improve the model behavior greatly by combining technological changes with value changes that reduce the growth tendencies of the system. Different combinations of such policies give us a series of computer outputs that represent a system with reasonably high values of industrial output per capita and with long-term stability. One example of such an output is shown in figure 46.

The policies that produced the behavior shown in figure 46 are:

1. Population is stabilized by setting the birth rate equal to the death rate in 1975. Industrial capital is allowed to increase naturally until 1990, after which it, too, is stabilized, by setting the investment rate equal to the depreciation rate.

2. To avoid a nonrenewable resource shortage such as that shown in figure 45, resource consumption per unit of industrial output is reduced to one-fourth of its 1970 value. (This and the following five policies are introduced in 1975.)

3. To further reduce resource depletion and pollution, the economic preferences of society are shifted more toward services such as education and health facilities and less toward factory-produced material goods. (This change is made through the relationship giving "indicated" or "desired" services per capita as a function of rising income.)

4. Pollution generation per unit of industrial and agricultural output is reduced to one-fourth of its 1970 value.

5. Since the above policies alone would result in a rather low value of food per capita, some people would still be malnourished if the traditional inequalities of distribution persist. To avoid this situation, high value is placed on producing sufficient food for *all* people. Capital is therefore diverted to food production even if such an investment would be considered "uneconomic." (This change is carried out through the "indicated" food per capita relationship.)

6. This emphasis on highly capitalized agriculture, while necessary to produce enough food, would lead to rapid soil erosion and depletion of soil fertility, destroying long-term stability in the agricultural sector. Therefore the use of agricultural capital has been altered to make soil enrichment and preservation a high priority. This policy implies, for example, use of capital to compost urban organic wastes and return them to the land (a practice that also reduces pollution).

7. The drains on industrial capital for higher services and food production and for resource recycling and pollution control under the above six conditions would lead to a low final level of industrial capital stock. To counteract this effect, the average lifetime of industrial capital is increased, implying better design for durability and repair and less discarding because of obsolescence. This policy also tends to reduce resource depletion and pollution.

In figure 46 the stable world population is only slightly larger than the population today. There is more than twice as much food per person as the average value in 1970, and world average lifetime is about 75 years. The average indus-

Figure 46 STABILIZED WORLD MODEL I

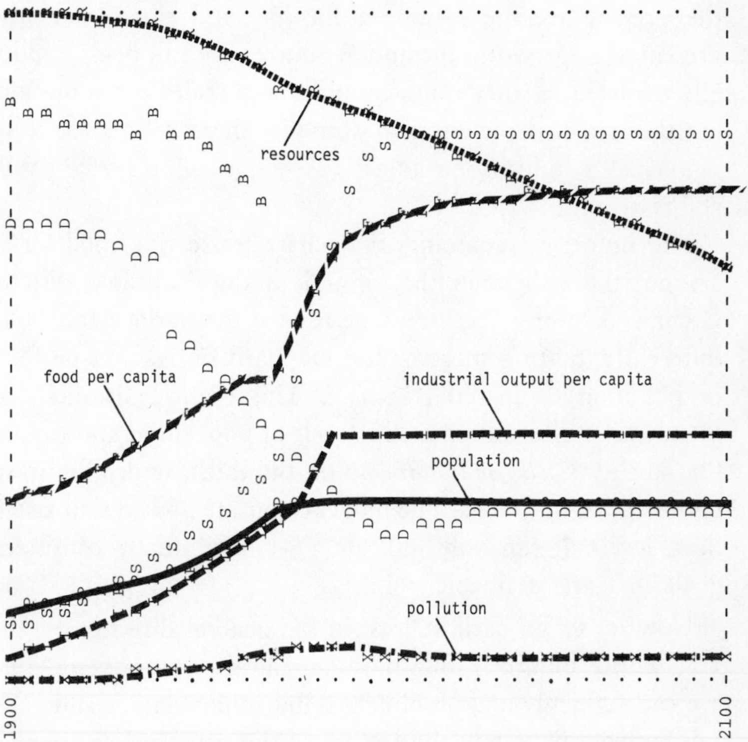

Technological policies are added to the growth-regulating policies of the previous run to produce an equilibrium state sustainable far into the future. Technological policies include resource recycling, pollution control devices, increased lifetime of all forms of capital, and methods to restore eroded and infertile soil. Value changes include increased emphasis on food and services rather than on industrial production. As in figure 45, births are set equal to deaths and industrial capital investment equal to capital depreciation. Equilibrium value of industrial output per capita is three times the 1970 world average.

trial output per capita is well above today's level, and services per capita have tripled. Total average income per capita (industrial output, food, and services combined) is about $1,800. This value is about half the present average US income, equal to the present average European income, and three times the present average world income. Resources are still being gradually depleted, as they must be under any realistic assumption, but the rate of depletion is so slow that there is time for technology and industry to adjust to changes in resource availability.

The numerical constants that characterize this model run are not the only ones that would produce a stable system. Other people or societies might resolve the various trade-offs differently, putting more or less emphasis on services or food or pollution or material income. This example is included merely as an illustration of the levels of population and capital that are *physically maintainable* on the earth, under the most optimistic assumptions. The model cannot tell us how to attain these levels. It can only indicate a set of mutually consistent goals that are attainable.

Now let us go back at least in the general direction of the real world and relax our most unrealistic assumptions—that we can suddenly and absolutely stabilize population and capital. Suppose we retain the last six of the seven policy changes that produced figure 46, but replace the first policy, beginning in 1975, with the following:

1. The population has access to 100 percent effective birth control.

2. The average desired family size is two children.

3. The economic system endeavors to maintain average industrial output per capita at about the 1975 level. Excess industrial capability is employed for producing consumption goods rather than increasing the industrial capital investment rate above the depreciation rate.

The model behavior that results from this change is shown in figure 47. Now the delays in the system allow population to grow larger than it did in figure 46. As a consequence, material goods, food, and services per capita remain lower than in previous runs (but still higher than they are on a world average today).

We do not suppose that any single one of the policies necessary to attain system stability in the model can or should be suddenly introduced in the world by 1975. A society choosing stability as a goal certainly must approach that goal gradually. It is important to realize, however, that the longer exponential growth is allowed to continue, the fewer possibilities remain for the final stable state. Figure 48 shows the result of waiting until the year 2000 to institute the same policies that were instituted in 1975 in figure 47.

In figure 48 both population and industrial output per capita reach much higher values than in figure 47. As a result pollution builds to a higher level and resources are severely depleted, in spite of the resource-saving policies finally introduced. In fact, during the 25-year delay (from 1975 to 2000) in instituting the stabilizing policies, resource consumption is about equal to the total 125-year consumption from 1975 to 2100 of figure 47.

Many people will think that the changes we have introduced into the model to avoid the growth-and-collapse behavior mode are not only impossible, but unpleasant, dangerous, even disastrous in themselves. Such policies as reducing the birth rate and diverting capital from production of material goods, by whatever means they might be implemented, seem unnatural and unimaginable, because they have not, in most people's experience, been tried, or even seriously suggested. Indeed there

Figure 47 STABILIZED WORLD MODEL II

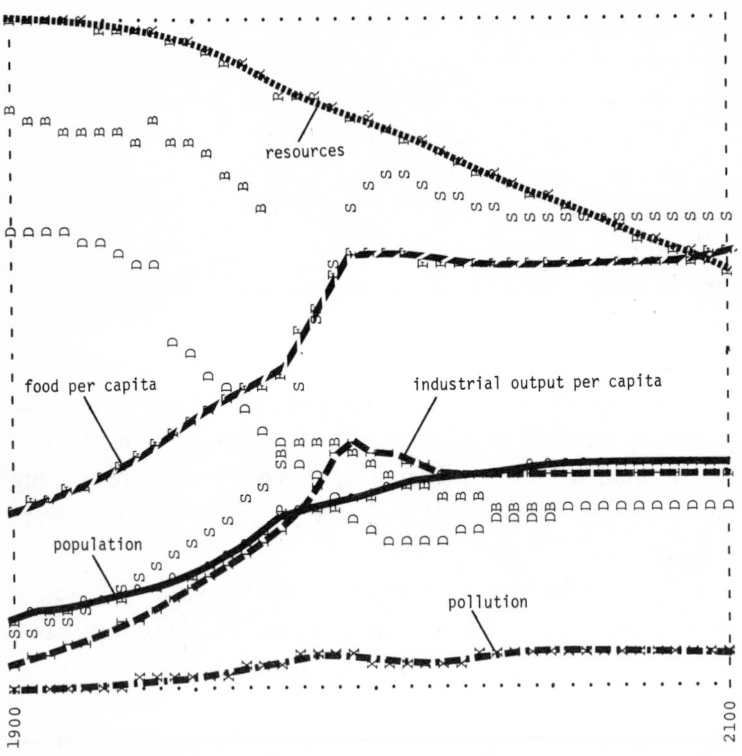

If the strict restrictions on growth of the previous run are removed, and population and capital are regulated within the natural delays of the system, the equilibrium level of population is higher and the level of industrial output per capita is lower than in figure 46. Here it is assumed that perfectly effective birth control and an average desired family size of two children are achieved by 1975. The birth rate only slowly approaches the death rate because of delays inherent in the age structure of the population.

would be little point even in discussing such fundamental changes in the functioning of modern society if we felt that the present pattern of unrestricted growth were sustainable into the future. All the evidence available to us, however, suggests that of the three alternatives—unrestricted growth, a self-

Figure 48 WORLD MODEL WITH STABILIZING POLICIES INTRODUCED IN THE YEAR 2000

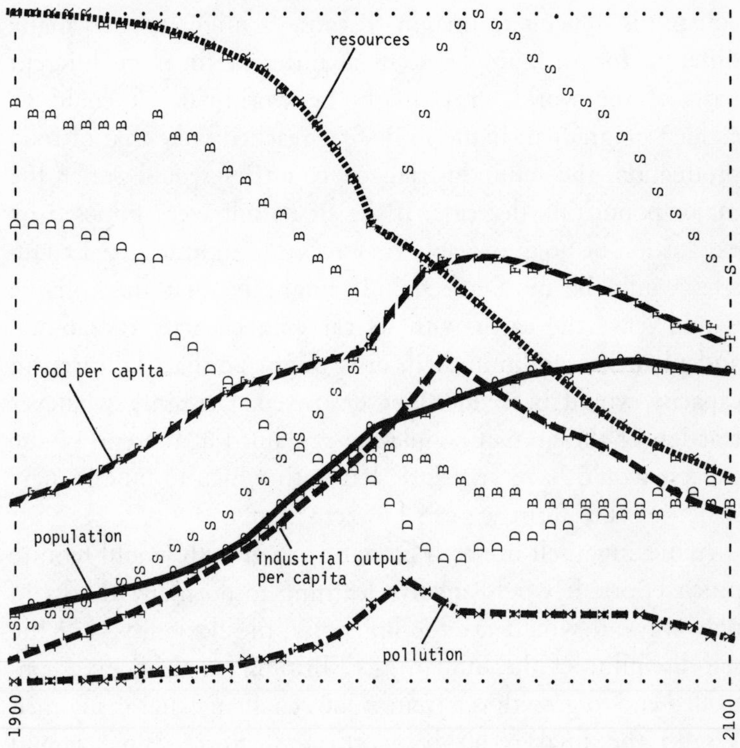

If all the policies instituted in 1975 in the previous figure are delayed until the year 2000, the equilibrium state is no longer sustainable. Population and industrial capital reach levels high enough to create food and resource shortages before the year 2100.

imposed limitation to growth, or a nature-imposed limitation to growth—only the last two are actually possible.

Accepting the nature-imposed limits to growth requires no more effort than letting things take their course and waiting to see what will happen. The most probable result of that decision, as we have tried to show here, will be an uncontrollable decrease in population and capital. The real meaning of such a collapse is difficult to imagine because it might take so many different forms. It might occur at different times in different parts of the world, or it might be worldwide. It could be sudden or gradual. If the limit first reached were that of food production, the nonindustrialized countries would suffer the major population decrease. If the first limit were imposed by exhaustion of nonrenewable resources, the industrialized countries would be most affected. It might be that the collapse would leave the earth with its carrying capacity for animal and plant life undiminished, or it might be that the carrying capacity would be reduced or destroyed. Certainly whatever fraction of the human population remained at the end of the process would have very little left with which to build a new society in any form we can now envision.

Achieving a self-imposed limitation to growth would require much effort. It would involve learning to do many things in new ways. It would tax the ingenuity, the flexibility, and the self-discipline of the human race. Bringing a deliberate, controlled end to growth is a tremendous challenge, not easily met. Would the final result be worth the effort? What would humanity gain by such a transition, and what would it lose? Let us consider in more detail what a world of nongrowth might be like.

THE EQUILIBRIUM STATE

We are by no means the first people in man's written history to propose some sort of nongrowing state for human society. A number of philosophers, economists, and biologists have discussed such a state and called it by many different names, with as many different meanings.*

We have, after much discussion, decided to call the state of constant population and capital, shown in figures 46 and 47, by the term "equilibrium." Equilibrium means a state of balance or equality between opposing forces. In the dynamic terms of the world model, the opposing forces are those causing population and capital stock to increase (high desired family size, low birth control effectiveness, high rate of capital investment) and those causing population and capital stock to decrease (lack of food, pollution, high rate of depreciation or obsolescence). The word "capital" should be understood to mean service, industrial, and agricultural capital combined. *Thus the most basic definition of the state of global equilibrium is that population and capital are essentially stable, with the forces tending to increase or decrease them in a carefully controlled balance.*

There is much room for variation within that definition. We have only specified that the stocks of capital and population remain constant, but they might theoretically be constant

---

* See, for instance:

Plato, *Laws,* 350 B.C.

Aristotle, *Politics,* 322 B.C.

Thomas Robert Malthus, *An Essay on the Principle of Population,* 1798.

John Stuart Mill, *Principles of Political Economy,* 1857.

Harrison Brown, *The Challenge of Man's Future* (New York: Viking Press, 1954).

Kenneth E. Boulding, "The Economics of the Coming Spaceship Earth," in *Environmental Quality in a Growing Economy,* ed. H. Jarrett (Baltimore, Md.: Johns Hopkins Press, 1966).

E. J. Mishan, *The Costs of Economic Growth* (New York: Frederick A. Praeger, 1967).

Herman E. Daly, "Toward a Stationary-State Economy," in *The Patient Earth,* ed. J. Harte and Robert Socolow (New York: Holt, Rinehart, and Winston, 1971).

at a high level or a low level—or one might be high and the other low. A tank of water can be maintained at a given level with a fast inflow and outflow of water or with a slow trickle in and out. If the flow is fast, the average drop of water will spend less time in the tank than if the flow is slow. Similarly, a stable population of any size can be achieved with either high, equal birth and death rates (short average lifetime) or low, equal birth and death rates (long average lifetime). A stock of capital can be maintained with high investment and depreciation rates or low investment and depreciation rates. Any combination of these possibilities would fit into our basic definition of global equilibrium.

What criteria can be used to choose among the many options available in the equilibrium state? The dynamic interactions in the world system indicate that the first decision that must be made concerns time. *How long should the equilibrium state exist?* If society is only interested in a time span of 6 months or a year, the world model indicates that almost any level of population and capital could be maintained. If the time horizon is extended to 20 or 50 years, the options are greatly reduced, since the rates and levels must be adjusted to ensure that the capital investment rate will not be limited by resource availability during that time span, or that the death rate will not be uncontrollably influenced by pollution or food shortage. The longer a society prefers to maintain the state of equilibrium, the lower the rates and levels must be.

At the limit, of course, no population or capital level can be maintained forever, but that limit is very far away in time if resources are managed wisely and if there is a sufficiently long time horizon in planning. Let us take as a reasonable time horizon the expected lifetime of a child born into the world tomorrow—70 years if proper food and medical care are supplied. Since most people spend a large part of their time and energy raising children, they might choose as a minimum goal that the society left to those children can be maintained for the full span of the children's lives.

If society's time horizon is as long as 70 years, the permissible population and capital levels may not be too different from those existing today, as indicated by the equilibrium run in figure 47 (which is, of course, only one of several possibilities). The rates would be considerably different from those of today, however. Any society would undoubtedly prefer that the death rate be low rather than high, since a long, healthy life seems to be a universal human desire. To maintain equilibrium with long life expectancy, the birth rate then must also be low. It would be best, too, if the capital investment and depreciation rates were low, because the lower they are, the less resource depletion and pollution there will be. Keeping depletion and pollution to a minimum could either increase the maximum size of the population and capital levels or increase the length of time the equilibrium state could be maintained, depending on which goal the society as a whole preferred.

By choosing a fairly long time horizon for its existence, and a long average lifetime as a desirable goal, we have now arrived at a minimum set of requirements for the state of global equilibrium. They are:

1. *The capital plant and the population are constant in size.* The birth rate equals the death rate and the capital investment rate equals the depreciation rate.

2. *All input and output rates—births, deaths, investment, and depreciation—are kept to a minimum.*

3. *The levels of capital and population and the ratio of the two are set in accordance with the values of the society.* They may be deliberately revised and slowly adjusted as the advance of technology creates new options.

An equilibrium defined in this way does not mean stagnation. Within the first two guidelines above, corporations could expand or fail, local populations could increase or decrease, income could become more or less evenly distributed. Technological advance would permit the services provided by a constant stock of capital to increase slowly. Within the third guideline, any country could change its average standard of living by altering the balance between its population and its capital. Furthermore, a society could adjust to changing internal or external factors by raising or lowering the population or capital stocks, or both, slowly and in a controlled fashion, with a predetermined goal in mind. The three points above define a *dynamic* equilibrium, which need not and probably would not "freeze" the world into the population-capital configuration that happens to exist at the present time. The object in accepting the above three statements is to create freedom for society, not to impose a straitjacket.

What would life be like in such an equilibrium state? Would innovation be stifled? Would society be locked into the patterns of inequality and injustice we see in the world today? Discussion of these questions must proceed on the basis of mental models, for there is no formal model of social conditions in the equilibrium state. No one can predict what sort of institutions mankind might develop under these new conditions. There is, of course, no guarantee that the new society would be much better or even much different from that which exists today. It seems possible, however, that a society released from struggling with the many problems caused by growth may have more energy and ingenuity available for solving other problems. In fact, we believe, as we will illustrate below, that the evolution of a society that favors innovation and technological development, a society based on equality and justice, is far more likely to evolve in a state of global equilibrium than it is in the state of growth we are experiencing today.

GROWTH IN THE EQUILIBRIUM STATE

In 1857 John Stuart Mill wrote:

> It is scarcely necessary to remark that a stationary condition of capital and population implies no stationary state of human improvement. There would be as much scope as ever for all kinds of mental culture, and moral and social progress; as much room for improving the Art of Living and much more likelihood of its being improved.[49]

Population and capital are the only quantities that need be constant in the equilibrium state. Any human activity that does not require a large flow of irreplaceable resources or produce severe environmental degradation might continue to grow indefinitely. In particular, those pursuits that many people would list as the most desirable and satisfying activities of man—education, art, music, religion, basic scientific research, athletics, and social interactions—could flourish.

All of the activities listed above depend very strongly on two factors. First, they depend upon the availability of some surplus production after the basic human needs of food and shelter have been met. Second, they require leisure time. In any equilibrium state the relative levels of capital and population could be adjusted to assure that human material needs are fulfilled at any desired level. Since the amount of material production would be essentially fixed, every improvement in production methods could result in increased leisure for the population—leisure that could be devoted to any activity that is relatively nonconsuming and nonpolluting, such as those listed above. Thus, this unhappy situation described by Bertrand Russell could be avoided:

> Suppose that, at a given moment, a certain number of people are engaged in the manufacture of pins. They make as many pins as the world needs, working (say) eight hours a day. Someone makes an invention by which the same number of men can make twice as many pins as before. But the world does not need twice as many pins. Pins are already so cheap that hardly any more will be bought at a lower price. In a sensible world, everybody concerned in the manufacture of pins would take to working four hours instead of eight, and everything else would go on as before. But in the actual world this would be thought demoralizing. The men still work eight hours, there are too many pins, some employers go bankrupt, and half the men previously concerned in making pins are thrown out of work. There is, in the end, just as much leisure as on the other plan, but half the men are totally idle while half are still overworked. In this way it is insured that the unavoidable leisure shall cause misery all around instead of being a universal source of happiness. Can anything more insane be imagined? [50]

But would the technological improvements that permit the production of pins or anything else more efficiently be forthcoming in a world where all basic material needs are fulfilled and additional production is not allowed? Does man have to be pushed by hardship and the incentive of material growth to devise better ways to do things?

Historical evidence would indicate that very few key inventions have been made by men who had to spend all their energy overcoming the immediate pressures of survival. Atomic energy was discovered in the laboratories of basic science by individuals unaware of any threat of fossil fuel depletion. The first genetic experiments, which led a hundred years later to high-yield agricultural crops, took place in the peace of a European monastery. Pressing human need may have forced the application of these basic discoveries to practical problems, but only freedom from need produced the knowledge necessary for the practical applications.

Technological advance would be both necessary and welcome in the equilibrium state. A few obvious examples of the kinds of practical discoveries that would enhance the workings of a steady state society include:

- new methods of waste collection, to decrease pollution and make discarded material available for recycling;
- more efficient techniques of recycling, to reduce rates of resource depletion;
- better product design to increase product lifetime and promote easy repair, so that the capital depreciation rate would be minimized;
- harnessing of incident solar energy, the most pollution-free power source;
- methods of natural pest control, based on more complete understanding of ecological interrelationships;
- medical advances that would decrease the death rate;
- contraceptive advances that would facilitate the equalization of the birth rate with the decreasing death rate.

As for the incentive that would encourage men to produce such technological advances, what better incentive could there be than the knowledge that a new idea would be translated into a visible improvement in the quality of life? Historically mankind's long record of new inventions has resulted in crowding, deterioration of the environment, and greater social inequality because greater productivity has been absorbed by population and capital growth. There is no reason why higher productivity could not be translated into a higher standard of living or more leisure or more pleasant surroundings for everyone, if these goals replace growth as the primary value of society.

EQUALITY IN THE EQUILIBRIUM STATE

One of the most commonly accepted myths in our present society is the promise that a continuation of our present patterns of growth will lead to human equality. We have demonstrated in various parts of this book that present patterns of population and capital growth are actually increasing the gap between the rich and the poor on a worldwide basis, and that the ultimate result of a continued attempt to grow according to the present pattern will be a disastrous collapse.

The greatest possible impediment to more equal distribution of the world's resources is population growth. It seems to be a universal observation, regrettable but understandable, that, as the number of people over whom a fixed resource must be distributed increases, the equality of distribution decreases. Equal sharing becomes social suicide if the average amount available per person is not enough to maintain life. FAO studies of food distribution have actually documented this general observation.

> Analysis of distribution curves shows that when the food supplies of a group diminish, inequalities in intake are accentuated, while the number of undernourished families increases more than in proportion to the deviation from the mean. Moreover, the food intake deficit grows with the size of households so that large families, and their children in particular, are statistically the most likely to be underfed.[51]

In a long-term equilibrium state, the relative levels of population and capital, and their relationships to fixed constraints such as land, fresh water, and mineral resources, would have to be set so that there would be enough food and material production to maintain everyone at (at least) a subsistence level. One barrier to equal distribution would thus be removed. Furthermore, the other effective barrier to equality—the promise of growth—could no longer be maintained, as Dr. Herman E. Daly has pointed out:

> For several reasons the important issue of the stationary state will be distribution, not production. The problem of relative shares can no longer be avoided by appeals to growth. The argument that everyone should be happy as long as his absolute share of wealth increases, regardless of his relative share, will no longer be available. . . . The stationary state would make fewer demands on our environmental resources, but much greater demands on our moral resources.[52]

There is, of course, no assurance that humanity's moral resources would be sufficient to solve the problem of income distribution, even in an equilibrium state. However, there is even less assurance that such social problems will be solved in the present state of growth, which is straining both the moral and the physical resources of the world's people.

The picture of the equilibrium state we have drawn here is idealized, to be sure. It may be impossible to achieve in the form described here, and it may not be the form most people on earth would choose. The only purpose in describing it at all is to emphasize that global equilibrium need not mean an end to progress or human development. The possibilities within an equilibrium state are almost endless.

An equilibrium state would not be free of pressures, since no society can be free of pressures. Equilibrium would require trading certain human freedoms, such as producing unlimited numbers of children or consuming uncontrolled amounts of resources, for other freedoms, such as relief from pollution and crowding and the threat of collapse of the world system. It is possible that new freedoms might also arise—universal and unlimited education, leisure for creativity and inventiveness, and, most important of all, the freedom from hunger and poverty enjoyed by such a small fraction of the world's people today.

THE TRANSITION FROM GROWTH TO GLOBAL EQUILIBRIUM

We can say very little at this point about the practical, day-by-day steps that might be taken to reach a desirable, sustainable state of global equilibrium. Neither the world model nor our own thoughts have been developed in sufficient detail to understand all the implications of the transition from growth to equilibrium. Before any part of the world's society embarks deliberately on such a transition, there must be much more discussion, more extensive analysis, and many new ideas contributed by many different people. If we have stimulated each reader of this book to begin pondering how such a transition might be carried out, we have accomplished our immediate goal.

Certainly much more information is needed to manage the transition to global equilibrium. In the process of sifting the world's data and incorporating it into an organized model, we have become aware of the great need for more *facts*—for numbers that are scientifically measurable but which have not yet been measured. The most glaring deficiencies in present knowledge occur in the pollution sector of the model. How long does it take for any given pollutant to travel from its point of release to its point of entrance into the human body? Does the time required for the processing of any pollutant into harmless form depend on the level of pollutant? Do several different pollutants acting together have a synergistic effect on human health? What are the long-term effects of low-level dosages on humans and other organisms? There is also a need for more information about rates of soil erosion and land wastage under intensified modern agricultural practices.

From our own vantage point as systems analysts, of course, we would recommend that the search for facts not be random but be governed by a greatly increased emphasis on establishing *system structure.* The behavior of all complicated social systems is primarily determined by the web of physical, biological, psychological, and economic relationships that binds together any human population, its natural environment, and its economic activities. Until the underlying structures of our socioeconomic systems are thoroughly analyzed, they cannot be managed effectively, just as an automobile cannot be maintained in good running condition without a knowledge of how its many parts influence each other. Studies of system structure may reveal that the introduction into a system of some simple stabilizing feedback mechanism will solve many difficulties. There have been interesting suggestions along that line already—for example, that the total costs of pollution and resource depletion be included in the price of a product, or that every user of river water be required to place his intake pipe *downstream* from his effluent pipe.

The final, most elusive, and most important information we need deals with human values. As soon as a society recognizes that it cannot maximize everything for everyone, it must begin to make choices. Should there be more people or more wealth, more wilderness or more automobiles, more food for the poor or more services for the rich? Establishing the societal answers to questions like these and translating those answers into policy is the essence of the political process. Yet few people in any society even realize that such choices are being made every day, much less ask themselves what their own choices would be. The equilibrium society will have to weigh the trade-offs engendered by a finite earth not only with consideration of present human values but also with consideration of future generations. To do that, society will need better means than exist today for clarifying the realistic alternatives available, for establishing societal goals, and for achieving the alternatives that are most consistent with those goals. But most important of all, long-term goals must be specified and short-term goals made consistent with them.

Although we underline the need for more study and discussion of these difficult questions, we end on a note of urgency. We hope that intensive study and debate will proceed simultaneously with an ongoing program of action. The details are not yet specified, but the general direction for action is obvious. Enough is known already to analyze many proposed policies in terms of their tendencies to promote or to regulate growth. Numerous nations have adopted or are considering programs to stabilize their populations. Some localized areas are also trying to reduce their rates of economic growth.[53] These efforts are weak at the moment, but they could be strengthened very quickly if the goal of equilibrium were recognized as desirable and important by any sizable part of human society.

We have repeatedly emphasized the importance of the natural delays in the population-capital system of the world. These delays mean, for example, that if Mexico's birth rate gradually declined from its present value to an exact replacement value by the year 2000, the country's population would continue to grow until the year 2060. During that time the population would grow from 50 million to 130 million.[54] If the United States population had two children per family starting now and if there were no net immigration, the population would still continue to grow until the year 2037, and it would increase from 200 million to 266 million.[55] If world population as a whole reached a replacement-size family by the year 2000 (at which time the population would be 5.8 billion), the delays caused by the age structure would result in a final leveling-off of population at 8.2 billion[56] (assuming that the death rate would not rise before then—an unlikely assumption, according to our model results).

Taking no action to solve these problems is equivalent to taking strong action. Every day of continued exponential growth brings the world system closer to the ultimate limits to that growth. A decision to do nothing is a decision to increase the risk of collapse. We cannot say with certainty how much longer mankind can postpone initiating deliberate control of his growth before he will have lost the chance for control. We suspect on the basis of present knowledge of the physical constraints of the planet that the growth phase cannot continue for another one hundred years. Again, because of the delays in the system, if the global society waits until those constraints are unmistakably apparent, it will have waited too long.

If there is cause for deep concern, there is also cause for hope. Deliberately limiting growth would be difficult, but not impossible. The way to proceed is clear, and the necessary steps, although they are new ones for human society, are well within human capabilities. Man possesses, for a small moment in his history, the most powerful combination of knowledge, tools, and resources the world has ever known. He has all that is physically necessary to create a totally new form of human society—one that would be built to last for generations. The two missing ingredients are a realistic, long-term goal that can guide mankind to the equilibrium society and the human will to achieve that goal. Without such a goal and a commitment to it, short-term concerns will generate the exponential growth that drives the world system toward the limits of the earth and ultimate collapse. With that goal and that commitment, mankind would be ready now to begin a controlled, orderly transition from growth to global equilibrium.

COMMENTARY

In inviting the MIT team to undertake this investigation, we had two immediate objectives in mind. One was to gain insights into the limits of our world system and the constraints it puts on human numbers and activity. Nowadays, more than ever before, man tends toward continual, often accelerated, growth—of population, land occupancy, production, consumption, waste, etc.—blindly assuming that his environment will permit such expansion, that other groups will yield, or that science and technology will remove the obstacles. We wanted to explore the degree to which this attitude toward growth is compatible with the dimensions of our finite planet and with the fundamental needs of our emerging world society—from the reduction of social and political tensions to improvement in the quality of life for all.

A second objective was to help identify and study the dominant elements, and their interactions, that influence the long-term behavior of world systems. Such knowledge, we believe, cannot be gathered by concentrating on national systems and short-run analyses, as is the current practice. The project was not intended as a piece of futurology. It was intended to be, and is, an analysis of current trends, of their influence on each other, and of their possible outcomes. Our goal was to provide warnings of potential world crisis if these trends are allowed to continue, and thus offer an opportunity to make changes in our political, economic, and social systems to ensure that these crises do not take place.

The report has served these purposes well. It represents a bold step toward a comprehensive and integrated analysis of the world situation, an approach that will now require years to refine, deepen, and extend. Nevertheless, this report is only a first step. The limits to growth it examines are only the known uppermost physical limits imposed by the finiteness of the world system. In reality, these limits are further reduced by political, social, and institutional constraints, by inequitable distribution of population and resources, and by our inability to manage very large intricate systems.

But the report serves further purposes. It advances tentative suggestions for the future state of the world and opens new perspectives for continual intellectual and practical endeavor to shape that future.

We have presented the findings of this report at two international meetings. Both were held in the summer of 1971, one in Moscow and the other in Rio de Janeiro. Although there were many questions and criticisms raised, there was no substantial disagreement with the perspectives described in this report. A preliminary draft of the report was also submitted to some forty individuals, most of them members of The Club of Rome, for their comments. It may be of interest to mention some of the main points of criticism:

1. Since models can accommodate only a limited number of variables, the interactions studied are only partial. It was

pointed out that in a global model such as the one used in this study the degree of aggregation is necessarily high as well. Nevertheless, it was generally recognized that, with a simple world model, it is possible to examine the effect of a change in basic assumptions or to simulate the effect of a change in policy to see how such changes influence the behavior of the system over time. Similar experimentation in the real world would be lengthy, costly, and in many cases impossible.

2. It was suggested that insufficient weight had been given to the possibilities of scientific and technological advances in solving certain problems, such as the development of foolproof contraceptive methods, the production of protein from fossil fuels, the generation or harnessing of virtually limitless energy (including pollution-free solar energy), and its subsequent use for synthesizing food from air and water and for extracting minerals from rocks. It was agreed, however, that such developments would probably come too late to avert demographic or environmental disaster. In any case they probably would only delay rather than avoid crisis, for the problematique consists of issues that require more than technical solutions.

3. Others felt that the possibility of discovering stocks of raw materials in areas as yet insufficiently explored was much greater than the model assumed. But, again, such discoveries would only postpone shortage rather than eliminate it. It must, however, be recognized that extension of resource availability by several decades might give man time to find remedies.

4. Some considered the model too "technocratic," observing that it did not include critical social factors, such as the effects of adoption of different value systems. The chairman of the

Moscow meeting summed up this point when he said, "Man is no mere biocybernetic device." This criticism is readily admitted. The present model considers man only in his material system because valid social elements simply could not be devised and introduced in this first effort. Yet, despite the model's material orientation, the conclusions of the study point to the need for fundamental change in the values of society.

Overall, a majority of those who read this report concurred with its position. Furthermore, it is clear that, if the arguments submitted in the report (even after making allowance for justifiable criticism) are considered valid in principle, their significance can hardly be overestimated.

Many reviewers shared our belief that the essential significance of the project lies in its global concept, for it is through knowledge of wholes that we gain understanding of components, and not vice versa. The report presents in straightforward form the alternatives confronting not one nation or people but all nations and all peoples, thereby compelling a reader to raise his sights to the dimensions of the world problematique. A drawback of this approach is of course that —given the heterogeneity of world society, national political structures, and levels of development—the conclusions of the study, although valid for our planet as a whole, do not apply in detail to any particular country or region.

It is true that in practice events take place in the world sporadically at points of stress—not generally or simultaneously throughout the planet. So, even if the consequences anticipated by the model were, through human inertia and political difficulties, allowed to occur, they would no doubt appear first in a series of local crises and disasters.

But it is probably no less true that these crises would have repercussions worldwide and that many nations and people, by taking hasty remedial action or retreating into isolationism and attempting self-sufficiency, would but aggravate the conditions operating in the system as a whole. The interdependence of the various components of the world system would make such measures futile in the end. War, pestilence, a raw materials starvation of industrial economies, or a generalized economic decay would lead to contagious social disintegration.

Finally, the report was considered particularly valuable in pointing out the exponential nature of human growth within a closed system, a concept rarely mentioned or appreciated in practical politics in spite of its immense implications for the future of our finite planet. The MIT project gives a reasoned and systematic explanation of trends of which people are but dimly aware.

The pessimistic conclusions of the report have been and no doubt will continue to be a matter for debate. Many will believe that, in population growth, for instance, nature will take remedial action, and birth rates will decline before catastrophe threatens. Others may simply feel that the trends identified in the study are beyond human control; these people will wait for "something to turn up." Still others will hope that minor corrections in present policies will lead to a gradual and satisfactory readjustment and possibly to equilibrium. And a great many others are apt to put their trust in technology, with its supposed cornucopia of cure-all solutions.

We welcome and encourage this debate. It is important, in our opinion, to ascertain the true scale of the crisis confronting mankind and the levels of severity it is likely to reach during the next decades.

From the response to the draft report we distributed, we

believe this book will cause a growing number of people throughout the world to ask themselves in earnest whether the momentum of present growth may not overshoot the carrying capacity of this planet—and to consider the chilling alternatives such an overshoot implies for ourselves, our children, and our grandchildren.

How do we, the sponsors of this project, evaluate the report? We cannot speak definitively for all our colleagues in The Club of Rome, for there are differences of interest, emphasis, and judgment among them. But, despite the preliminary nature of the report, the limits of some of its data, and the inherent complexity of the world system it attempts to describe, we are convinced of the importance of its main conclusions. We believe that it contains a message of much deeper significance than a mere comparison of dimensions, a message relevant to all aspects of the present human predicament.

Although we can here express only our preliminary views, recognizing that they still require a great deal of reflection and ordering, we are in agreement on the following points:

1. We are convinced that realization of the quantitative restraints of the world environment and of the tragic consequences of an overshoot is essential to the initiation of new forms of thinking that will lead to a fundamental revision of human behavior and, by implication, of the entire fabric of present-day society.

It is only now that, having begun to understand something of the interactions between demographic growth and economic growth, and having reached unprecedented levels in both, man is forced to take account of the limited dimensions of his planet and the ceilings to his presence and activity on it. For the first time, it has become vital to inquire into the cost of unrestricted material growth and to consider alternatives to its continuation.

2. We are further convinced that demographic pressure in the world has already attained such a high level, and is moreover so unequally distributed, that this alone must compel mankind to seek a state of equilibrium on our planet.

Underpopulated areas still exist; but, considering the world as a whole, the critical point in population growth is approaching, if it has not already been reached. There is of course no unique optimum, long-term population level; rather, there are a series of balances between population levels, social and material standards, personal freedom, and other elements making up the quality of life. Given the finite and diminishing stock of nonrenewable resources and the finite space of our globe, the principle must be generally accepted that growing numbers of people will eventually imply a lower standard of living—and a more complex problematique. On the other hand, no fundamental human value would be endangered by a leveling off of demographic growth.

3. We recognize that world equilibrium can become a reality only if the lot of the so-called developing countries is substantially improved, both in absolute terms and relative to the economically developed nations, and we affirm that this improvement can be achieved only through a global strategy.

Short of a world effort, today's already explosive gaps and inequalities will continue to grow larger. The outcome can only be disaster, whether due to the selfishness of individual countries that continue to act purely in their own interests, or to a power struggle between the developing and developed nations. The world system is simply not ample enough nor generous enough to accommodate much longer such egocentric and conflictive behavior by its inhabitants. The closer we come to the material limits to the planet, the more difficult this problem will be to tackle.

4. We affirm that the global issue of development is, however, so closely interlinked with other global issues that an overall strategy must be evolved to attack all major problems, including in particular those of man's relationship with his environment.

With world population doubling time a little more than 30 years, and decreasing, society will be hard put to meet the needs and expectations of so many more people in so short a period. We are likely to try to satisfy these demands by overexploiting our natural environment and further impairing the life-supporting capacity of the earth. Hence, on both sides of the man-environment equation, the situation will tend to worsen dangerously. We cannot expect technological solutions alone to get us out of this vicious circle. The strategy for dealing with the two key issues of development and environment must be conceived as a joint one.

5. We recognize that the complex world problematique is to a great extent composed of elements that cannot be expressed in measurable terms. Nevertheless, we believe that the predominantly quantitative approach used in this report is an indispensable tool for understanding the operation of the problematique. And we hope that such knowledge can lead to a mastery of its elements.

Although all major world issues are fundamentally linked,

no method has yet been discovered to tackle the whole effectively. The approach we have adopted can be extremely useful in reformulating our thinking about the entire human predicament. It permits us to define the balances that must exist within human society, and between human society and its habitat, and to perceive the consequences that may ensue when such balances are disrupted.

6. We are unanimously convinced that rapid, radical redressment of the present unbalanced and dangerously deteriorating world situation is the primary task facing humanity.

Our present situation is so complex and is so much a reflection of man's multiple activities, however, that no combination of purely technical, economic, or legal measures and devices can bring substantial improvement. Entirely new approaches are required to redirect society toward goals of equilibrium rather than growth. Such a reorganization will involve a supreme effort of understanding, imagination, and political and moral resolve. We believe that the effort is feasible and we hope that this publication will help to mobilize forces to make it possible.

7. This supreme effort is a challenge for our generation. It cannot be passed on to the next. The effort must be resolutely undertaken without delay, and significant redirection must be achieved during this decade.

Although the effort may initially focus on the implications of growth, particularly of population growth, the totality of the world problematique will soon have to be addressed. We believe in fact that the need will quickly become evident for social innovation to match technical change, for radical reform of institutions and political processes at all levels, including the highest, that of world polity. We are confident that our generation will accept this challenge if we understand the tragic consequences that inaction may bring.

8. We have no doubt that if mankind is to embark on a new course, concerted international measures and joint long-term planning will be necessary on a scale and scope without precedent.

Such an effort calls for joint endeavor by all peoples, whatever their culture, economic system, or level of development. But the major responsibility must rest with the more developed nations, not because they have more vision or humanity, but because, having propagated the growth syndrome, they are still at the fountainhead of the progress that sustains it. As greater insights into the condition and workings of the world system are developed, these nations will come to realize that, in a world that fundamentally needs stability, their high plateaus of development can be justified or tolerated only if they serve not as springboards to reach even higher, but as staging areas from which to organize more equitable distribution of wealth and income worldwide.

9. We unequivocally support the contention that a brake imposed on world demographic and economic growth spirals must not lead to a freezing of the *status quo* of economic development of the world's nations.

If such a proposal were advanced by the rich nations, it would be taken as a final act of neocolonialism. The achievement of a harmonious state of global economic, social, and ecological equilibrium must be a joint venture based on joint conviction, with benefits for all. The greatest leadership will be demanded from the economically developed countries, for the first step toward such a goal would be for them to encourage a deceleration in the growth of their own material output while, at the same time, assisting the developing nations in their efforts to advance their economies more rapidly.

10. We affirm finally that any deliberate attempt to reach a rational and enduring state of equilibrium by planned measures, rather than by chance or catastrophe, must ultimately be founded on a basic change of values and goals at individual, national, and world levels.

This change is perhaps already in the air, however faintly. But our tradition, education, current activities, and interests will make the transformation embattled and slow. Only real comprehension of the human condition at this turning point in history can provide sufficient motivation for people to accept the individual sacrifices and the changes in political and economic power structures required to reach an equilibrium state.

The question remains of course whether the world situation is in fact as serious as this book, and our comments, would indicate. We firmly believe that the warnings this book contains are amply justified, and that the aims and actions of our present civilization can only aggravate the problems of tomorrow. But we would be only too happy if our tentative assessments should prove too gloomy.

In any event, our posture is one of very grave concern, but not of despair. The report describes an alternative to unchecked and disastrous growth and puts forward some thoughts on the policy changes that could produce a stable equilibrium for mankind. The report indicates that it may be within our reach to provide reasonably large populations with a good material life plus opportunities for limitless individual and social development. We are in substantial agreement with that view, although we are realistic enough not to be carried away by purely scientific or ethical speculations.

The concept of a society in a steady state of economic and ecological equilibrium may appear easy to grasp, although the reality is so distant from our experience as to require a Copernican revolution of the mind. Translating the idea into deed, though, is a task filled with overwhelming difficulties and complexities. We can talk seriously about where to start only when the message of *The Limits to Growth,* and its sense of extreme urgency, are accepted by a large body of scientific, political, and popular opinion in many countries. The transition in any case is likely to be painful, and it will make extreme demands on human ingenuity and determination. As we have mentioned, only the conviction that there is no other avenue to survival can liberate the moral, intellectual, and creative forces required to initiate this unprecedented human undertaking.

But we wish to underscore the challenge rather than the difficulty of mapping out the road to a stable state society. We believe that an unexpectedly large number of men and women of all ages and conditions will readily respond to the challenge and will be eager to discuss not *if* but *how* we can create this new future.

The Club of Rome plans to support such activity in many ways. The substantive research begun at MIT on world dynamics will be continued both at MIT and through studies conducted in Europe, Canada, Latin America, the Soviet Union, and Japan. And, since intellectual enlightenment is without effect if it is not also political, The Club of Rome also will encourage the creation of a world forum where statesmen, policy-makers, and scientists can discuss the dangers and hopes for the future global system without the constraints of formal intergovernmental negotiation.

The last thought we wish to offer is that man must explore himself—his goals and values—as much as the world he seeks to change. The dedication to both tasks must be unending. The crux of the matter is not only whether the human species will survive, but even more whether it can survive without falling into a state of worthless existence.

The Executive Committee of The Club of Rome

ALEXANDER KING
SABURO OKITA
AURELIO PECCEI
EDUARD PESTEL
HUGO THIEMANN
CARROLL WILSON

APPENDIX: Related Studies

Papers related to the MIT System Dynamics Group–Club of Rome Project on the Predicament of Mankind are listed below. An asterisk denotes each paper that is included in the second project report, Dennis L. Meadows and Donella H. Meadows (eds.), Toward Global Equilibrium *(Cambridge, Mass.: Wright-Allen Press, 1973).*

*ANDERSON, ALISON and ANDERSON, JAY M. "System Simulation to Test Environmental Policy III: The Flow of Mercury through the Environment." Mimeographed. Cambridge, Mass.: Massachusetts Institute of Technology, 1971.

*ANDERSON, JAY M. "System Simulation to Test Environmental Policy II: The Eutrophication of Lakes." Mimeographed. Cambridge, Mass.: Massachusetts Institute of Technology, 1971.

*BEHRENS, WILLIAM W. III. "The Dynamics of Natural Resource Utilization." Paper presented at the 1971 Summer Computer Simulation Conference, July 1971, Boston, Massachusetts, sponsored by the Board of Simulation Conferences, Denver, Colorado.

*BEHRENS, WILLIAM W. III and MEADOWS, DENNIS L. "The Determinants of Long-Term Resource Availability." Paper presented at the annual meeting of the American Association for the Advancement of Science, January 1971, Philadelphia, Pennsylvania.

CHOUCRI, NAZLI; LAIRD, MICHAEL; and MEADOWS, DENNIS L. "Resource Scarcity and Foreign Policy: A Simulation Model of International Conflict." Paper presented at the annual meeting of the American Association for the Advancement of Science, January 1971, Philadelphia, Pennsylvania.

* FORRESTER, JAY W. "Counterintuitive Nature of Social Systems." *Technology Review* 73 (1971): 53.

FORRESTER, JAY W. *World Dynamics.* Cambridge, Mass.: Wright-Allen Press, 1971.

HARBORDT, STEFFEN C. "Linking Socio-Political Factors to the World Model." Mimeographed. Cambridge, Mass.: Massachusetts Institute of Technology, 1971.

MEADOWS, DONELLA H. "The Dynamics of Population Growth in the Traditional Agricultural Village." Mimeographed. Cambridge, Mass.: Massachusetts Institute of Technology, 1971.

MEADOWS, DONELLA H. "Testimony Before the Education Committee of the Massachusetts Great and General Court on Behalf of the House Bill 3787." Republished as "Reckoning with Recklessness," *Ecology Today,* January 1972, p. 11.

MEADOWS, DENNIS L. *The Dynamics of Commodity Production Cycles.* Cambridge, Mass.: Wright-Allen Press, 1970.

* MEADOWS, DENNIS L. "MIT–Club of Rome Project on the Predicament of Mankind." Mimeographed. Cambridge, Mass.: Massachusetts Institute of Technology, 1971.

* MEADOWS, DENNIS L. "Some Requirements of a Successful Environmental Program." Hearings of the Subcommittee on Air and Water Pollution of the Senate Committee on Public Works, Part I, May 3, 1971. Washington, DC: Government Printing Office, 1971.

MILLING, PETER. "A Simple Analysis of Labor Displacement and Absorption in a Two Sector Economy." Mimeographed. Cambridge, Mass.: Massachusetts Institute of Technology, 1971.

*NAILL, ROGER F. "The Discovery Life Cycle of a Finite Resource: A Case Study of US Natural Gas." Mimeographed. Cambridge, Mass.: Massachusetts Institute of Technology, 1971.

*RANDERS, JØRGEN. "The Dynamics of Solid Waste Generation." Mimeographed. Cambridge, Mass.: Massachusetts Institute of Technology, 1971.

*RANDERS, JØRGEN and MEADOWS, DONELLA H. "The Carrying Capacity of our Global Environment: A Look at the Ethical Alternatives." In *Western Man and Environmental Ethics,* ed. Ian Barbour. Reading, Mass.: Addison-Wesley, 1972.

*RANDERS, JØRGEN and MEADOWS, DENNIS L. "System Simulation to Test Environmental Policy I: A Sample Study of DDT Movement in the Environment." Mimeographed. Cambridge, Mass.: Massachusetts Institute of Technology, 1971.

*SHANTZIS, STEPHEN B. and BEHRENS, WILLIAM W. III. "Population Control Mechanisms in a Primitive Agricultural Society." Mimeographed. Cambridge, Mass.: Massachusetts Institute of Technology, 1971.

NOTES

1. A. M. Carr-Saunders, *World Population: Past Growth and Present Trends* (Oxford: Clarendon Press, 1936), p. 42.

2. US Agency for International Development, *Population Program Assistance* (Washington, DC: Government Printing Office, 1970), p. 172.

3. *World Population Data Sheet 1968* (Washington, DC: Population Reference Bureau, 1968).

4. Lester R. Brown, *Seeds of Change* (New York: Praeger Publishers, 1970), p. 135.

5. President's Science Advisory Panel on the World Food Supply, *The World Food Problem* (Washington, DC: Government Printing Office, 1967) 2:5.

6. President's Science Advisory Panel on the World Food Supply, *The World Food Problem,* 2:423.

7. President's Science Advisory Panel on the World Food Supply, *The World Food Problem,* 2:460–69.

8. UN Food and Agriculture Organization, *Provisional Indicative World Plan for Agricultural Development* (Rome: UN Food and Agriculture Organization, 1970) 1:41.

9. Data from an Economic Research Service survey, reported by Rodney J. Arkley in "Urbanization of Agricultural Land in California," mimeographed (Berkeley, Calif.: University of California, 1970).

10. Paul R. Ehrlich and Anne H. Ehrlich, *Population, Resources, Environment* (San Francisco, Calif.: W. H. Freeman and Company, 1970), p. 72.

11. *Man's Impact on the Global Environment,* Report of the Study of Critical Environmental Problems (Cambridge, Mass.: MIT Press, 1970), p. 118.

12. *First Annual Report of the Council on Environmental Quality* (Washington, DC: Government Printing Office, 1970), p. 158.

13. US Bureau of Mines, *Mineral Facts and Problems, 1970* (Washington, DC: Government Printing Office, 1970), p. 247.

14. Mercury data from US Bureau of Mines, *Minerals Yearbook* (Washington, DC: Government Printing Office, 1967) 1(2):724 and US Bureau of Mines, *Commodity Data Summary* (Washington, DC: Government Printing Office, January 1971), p. 90. Lead data from *Metal Statistics* (Somerset, NJ: American Metal Market Company, 1970), p. 215.

15. G. Evelyn Hutchinson, "The Biosphere," *Scientific American,* September 1970, p. 53.

16. Chauncey Starr, "Energy and Power," *Scientific American,* September 1971, p. 42.

17. UN Department of Economic and Social Affairs, *Statistical Yearbook 1969* (New York: United Nations, 1970), p. 40.

18. Bert Bolin, "The Carbon Cycle," *Scientific American,* September 1970, p. 131.

19. *Inadvertent Climate Modification,* Report of the Study of Man's Impact on Climate (Cambridge, Mass.: MIT Press, 1971), p. 234.

20. John R. Clark, "Thermal Pollution and Aquatic Life," *Scientific American,* March 1969, p. 18.

21. *Inadvertent Climate Modification,* pp. 151–54.

22. John P. Holdren, "Global Thermal Pollution," in *Global Ecology,* ed. John P. Holdren and Paul R. Ehrlich (New York: Harcourt Brace Jovanovich, 1971), p. 85.

23. Baltimore Gas and Electric Company, "Preliminary Safety Analysis

Report," quoted in E. P. Ranford et al., "Statement of Concern," *Environment,* September 1969, p. 22.

24. R. A. Wallace, W. Fulkerson, W. D. Shults, and W. S. Lyons, *Mercury in the Environment* (Oak Ridge, Tenn.: Oak Ridge Laboratory, 1971).

25. *Man's Impact on the Global Environment,* p. 131.

26. C. C. Patterson and J. D. Salvia, "Lead in the Modern Environment," *Scientist and Citizen,* April 1968, p. 66.

27. *Second Annual Report of the Council on Environmental Quality* (Washington, DC: Government Printing Office, 1971), pp. 110-11.

28. Edward J. Kormandy, *Concepts of Ecology* (Englewood Cliffs, NJ: Prentice-Hall, 1969), pp. 95–97.

29. *Second Annual Report of the Council on Environmental Quality,* p. 105.

30. Calculated from average GNP per capita by means of relationships shown in H. B. Chenery and L. Taylor, "Development Patterns: Among Countries and Over Time," *Review of Economics and Statistics* 50 (1969): 391.

31. Calculated from data on metal and energy consumption in UN Department of Economic and Social Affairs, *Statistical Yearbook 1969.*

32. J. J. Spengler, "Values and Fertility Analysis," *Demography* 3 (1966): 109.

33. Lester B. Lave and Eugene P. Seskin, "Air Pollution and Human Health," *Science* 169 (1970): 723.

34. *Second Annual Report of the Council on Environmental Quality,* pp. 105–6.

35. Frank W. Notestein, "Zero Population Growth: What Is It?" *Family Planning Perspectives* 2 (June 1970): 20.

36. Donald J. Bogue, *Principles of Demography* (New York: John Wiley and Sons, 1969), p. 828.

37. R. Buckminster Fuller, *Comprehensive Design Strategy,* World Resources Inventory, Phase II (Carbondale, Ill.: University of Illinois, 1967), p. 48.

38. Thomas S. Lovering, "Mineral Resources from the Land," in Committee on Resources and Man, *Resources and Man* (San Francisco, Calif.: W. H. Freeman and Company, 1969), p. 122–23.

39. *Second Annual Report of the Council on Environmental Quality,* p. 118.

40. Garrett Hardin, "The Cybernetics of Competition: A Biologist's View of Society," *Perspectives in Biology and Medicine* 7 (Autumn 1963): 58, reprinted in Paul Shepard and Daniel McKinley, eds., *The Subversive Science* (Boston: Houghton Mifflin, 1969), p. 275.

41. S. R. Sen, *Modernizing Indian Agriculture* vol. 1, Expert Committee on Assessment and Evaluation (New Delhi: Ministry of Food, Agriculture, Community Development, and Cooperatives, 1969).

42. For an excellent summary of this problem see Robert d'A. Shaw, *Jobs and Agricultural Development,* (Washington, DC: Overseas Development Council, 1970).

43. Richard Critchfield, "It's a Revolution All Right," Alicia Patterson Fund paper (New York: Alicia Patterson Fund, 1971).

44. Robert d'A. Shaw, *Jobs and Agricultural Development,* p. 44.

45. Lester R. Brown, *Seeds of Change,* p. 112.

46. US Bureau of the Census, *1970 Census of Population and Housing, General Demographic Trends of Metropolitan Areas, 1960–70* (Washington, DC: Government Printing Office, 1971).

47. Garrett Hardin, "The Tragedy of the Commons," *Science* 162 (1968): 1243.

48. UN Food and Agriculture Organization, *The State of Food and Agriculture* (Rome: UN Food and Agriculture Organization, 1970), p. 6.

49. John Stuart Mill, *Principles of Political Economy,* in *The Collected Works of John Stuart Mill,* ed. V. W. Bladen and J. M. Robson (Toronto: University of Toronto Press, 1965), p. 754.

50. Bertrand Russell, *In Praise of Idleness and Other Essays* (London: Allen and Unwin, 1935), pp. 16–17.

51. UN Food and Agriculture Organization, *Provisional Indicative World Plan for Agricultural Development* 2: 490.

52. Herman E. Daly, "Toward a Stationary-State Economy," in *The Patient Earth,* ed. John Harte and Robert Socolow (New York: Holt, Rinehart, and Winston, 1971), pp. 236-37.

53. See, for example, "Fellow Americans Keep Out!" *Forbes,* June 15, 1971, p. 22, and *The Ecologist,* January 1972.

54. J. Bourgeois-Pichat and Si-Ahmed Taleb, "Un taux d'acroissement nul pour les pays en voie de developpement en l'an 2000: Reve ou realite?" *Population* 25 (September/October 1970): 957.

55. Commission on Population Growth and the American Future, *An Interim Report to the President and the Congress* (Washington, DC: Government Printing Office, 1971).

56. Bernard Berelson, *The Population Council Annual Report, 1970* (New York: The Population Council, 1970), p. 19.